5/18/95

Presented to:

Interboro Public Library

Peckville, PA

By

**A. PIERSON HURD
POST 236
PECKVILLE, PENNA.**

The History of the
PENNSYLVANIA AMERICAN LEGION

The History of the
PENNSYLVANIA
AMERICAN
LEGION

Terry Radtke

STACKPOLE
BOOKS

Published by
STACKPOLE BOOKS
5067 Ritter Road
Mechanicsburg, PA 17055

Printed in the United States of America

First Edition

10 9 8 7 6 5 4 3 2 1

Photographs courtesy of The American Legion National Headquarters Archives.

Library of Congress Cataloging-in-Publication Data

Radtke, Terry.
    The history of the Pennsylvania American Legion / Terry Radke—1st ed.
        p.   cm.
    Includes index.
    ISBN 0-8117-0818-7 : $19.95
    1. Pennsylvania American Legion—History   I. Title.
D570.A12P47   1993
369'.186—dc20   93-2535
                                                                    CIP

CONTENTS

143
APPENDICES

227
INDEX

PRESENT AT THE CREATION

Eric Fisher Wood and
Other Pennsylvania
Veterans in the Creation
of the American Legion

In January 1919, twenty citizen-officers of the American Expeditionary Force (AEF)—five of whom were Pennsylvanians—gathered on a winter evening at the Allied Officers' Club in the wake of the Great War.

The gathering, impressive by any measure, was at the behest of Theodore A. Roosevelt Jr. The dinner engagement, and especially the ensuing discussion, would be part of the history and myth of World War I.

The idea for what was to become the largest, most powerful, and certainly most controversial veterans' organization in American history officially developed out of the dinner held by the 26th president's oldest son. It was how he became known as the "Father of the American Legion." The Legion reflected the fusion of two kinds of organizations well represented throughout

1

the nation's past and present. First, as veterans *and* citizens, members' status was both special and vulnerable. Second, the Legion's eventual campaign for "100 Percent Americanism" brought back a mission taken up by veterans' groups from the early years of the republic. It would eventually link patriotism, a fervent opposition to radicalism, and a desire for stability once the veteran returned home.

William Pencak, in *For God and Country,* has shown that the American Legion was part of a tradition of veterans' organizations in America. From the founding of the nation, veterans have organized fraternal societies for three basic reasons. As men who had won and secured America's borders and unity, they saw themselves as charged with special obligations to preserve their achievements. To use the phrase of one of the American Legion's initial recruiting drives, they gathered "to keep the spirit of the Great War alive," curb the influence of anti-patriotic elements, and encourage a sense of national identity and unity among all classes and groups.

Veterans, however, had unique problems in American society. A nation that rewarded its heroes with honors and medals often also neglected to care for the disabled, widows, and orphans, or help the able-bodied adjust to civilian life. Finally, as Alexis de Tocqueville noted in his study of early American customs and life, people of all classes joined together to enjoy one another's company and renew a sense of "citizenship" by various community programs and activities.

The American Legion fits perfectly into the description of the nation's voluntary organizations given in Arthur Schlesinger Sr.'s 1944 article, "Biography of a Nation of Joiners." Such groups reached out "with interlocking memberships to all parts of the country, embracing all ages, classes, and creeds," and have served as the nation's "greatest school of self-government" and "one of the strongest taproots of the nation's well-being."

Given this background, it was reasonable to expect veterans of America's "Crusade for Democracy" to organize. Colonel Roosevelt made his proposal to prominent Reserve and National Guard officers for a veterans' association in which all members of the AEF would be eligible to join. Earlier, General Headquarters had requested that Roosevelt and nineteen other officers go to Paris in order to study the morale of the AEF's rank and file.

As representatives of various units, they also were to recommend a solution for what was assumed to be a growing morale problem among American troops. The Armistice had been signed approximately two months earlier on November 11, 1918. The impatience of many American servicemen, who demanded, "When do we sail?" and the problems of idleness were considered possible signs of greater unrest and mutiny.

Most of the young men (average age, twenty-five) in this morale conference shared a common background. They had spent their youth listening to the speeches of President Theodore Roosevelt and belonged to or attended the YMCA, Boy Scouts, and elite schools that encouraged idealism and a sense of sacrifice on behalf of the nation. After the war started in Europe in 1914, future Legionnaires joined "preparedness" societies whose goals and personnel eventually carried over into the American Legion. Some motivated individuals actually formed the first "American Legion" to gather the names of potential volunteers who had the military background and technical skills essential for war-time mobilization. By April 1917, the names of 50,000 prospective volunteers were given to the War Department. Others joined the Training Camps movement, founded three days after the sinking of the *Lusitania* on May 10, 1915. For the next three years, more than 20,000 men, some from Ivy League campuses and rather privileged backgrounds, paid $100 to attend these camps, the most famous of which was in Plattsburgh, New York. Four of the American Legion's organizers—"Wild Bill" Donovan, Theodore Roosevelt Jr., Hamilton Fish, and Eric Fisher Wood—were among the movement's principal founders. Virtually all of the "Plattsburghers" immediately enlisted once war was declared. These volunteers trained the nearly 200,000 Reserve officers who commanded most of the American forces in Europe.

On the first day of the morale conference, Colonel Roosevelt invited each participant to dine with him at the military club on the final evening in Paris. He said he wanted to discuss the formation of a veterans' organization or, as one participant described it, "The GAR of the World War." It was a reference to the Grand Army of the Republic, formed by Union Army veterans. Though veterans' groups from previous American wars had created a tradition that made the American Legion possible, the

GAR was its most practical model. As boys, future Legionnaires wrote of how they were moved when the veterans of the Civil War paraded on Memorial Day or reminisced about battles and campaigns. Enthusiasm for emulating the GAR went so far that in 1921, Legion Commander Hanford MacNider declared, "the Grand Army of the Republic dominated the United States for years after the Civil War, although it had but 20,000 members. What an opportunity for the American Legion!" Despite this exaggeration, similarities between the Legion and the GAR were striking; both united veterans to keep the spirit of their campaigns alive while working through political channels for benefits, pensions, and rehabilitation programs.

Colonel Roosevelt, a wounded combat veteran from the 1st Division, quickly won the group's support for his proposal. The group, in American Legion lore, would soon become known as the "Committee of Twenty." Two Pennsylvanians were in this cadre out of which would emerge the Legion's leadership: Lieutenant Colonels Eric Fisher Wood and Franklin D'Olier. These two colorful men were among the eleven officers who would work closely with Colonel Roosevelt to turn his vision into reality.

Pennsylvania's renowned 28th Infantry Division was important in the founding of the American Legion. Involved in the most significant engagements of the war, the Pennsylvania division suffered the heaviest casualties (14,000) of any National Guard unit. The 28th Division was more than adequately represented in early Legion gatherings. Several members of this unit were on the Committee of Twenty. For example, Lieutenant Colonel Fred W. Llewellyn, who before the war had been a brigadier general and adjutant general of the state of Washington, was assigned to the Keystone Division before joining General John J. Pershing's staff at General Headquarters. Lieutenant Colonel John Price Jackson, serving with the Peace Commission of the Wilson administration, also was a Pennsylvanian on the Committee of Twenty. Colonel David John Davis of Scranton, a member of Pershing's staff and former chief of staff of the 28th Division, became one of the first Pennsylvania Department commanders. He also served as lieutenant governor and state adjutant general.

D'Olier, a wealthy textile manufacturer from Philadelphia who organized the AEF's logistics system, was elected first national commander of the American Legion. He later headed one of the nation's largest life insurance and investment firms. Wood, perhaps the most immediately recognizable of Pennsylvania's contingent, was a temporary chairman and later was given the title of honorary national commander. An architect and engineer in civilian life, he designed the Legion emblem.

In many ways, Wood personified the spirit and elan of the Legion's early years. As a volunteer attaché at the American embassy in Paris, Wood glimpsed firsthand the diplomatic crisis that led to the outbreak of the war. Wood quickly joined the American Ambulance Corps in support of the Allied cause. He returned to the United States in 1915 and served as vice president of the preparedness-minded National Security League as well as a member of the Plattsburgh Training Camp Executive Committee. Wood then returned to the Western Front, where he served as a British army major. He was wounded at Arras in the spring of 1917. When war was declared on April 17, 1917, Wood was commissioned into the U.S. Army as assistant chief of staff for the 88th Division. Wood received a disabling poison gas injury during the Meuse-Argonne campaign. A Renaissance individual, Wood wrote constantly, publishing *Notebook of an Attaché* in 1915, *The Writing on the Wall* in 1916, and *The Notebook of an Intelligence Officer* after the war. He wrote regular features and stories about the war and Army life in *The Saturday Evening Post, The Times of London,* and many other publications. His introductory remarks at the Paris Conference became the philosophical guide to the preamble of the American Legion constitution.

Later critics of the Legion charged that the organization resulted from an officer-led plot. Wood contended that "the Legion was not initiated by a single individual, nor was it organized by any clique. It sprang into being as the result of a universal demand among the soldiers and sailors for an effective nationwide organization which would enable us to carry to the problems of peacetime the teamwork we had so well learned in time of war." Still, Wood and Roosevelt asserted later that they had created the Legion "out of our hip pockets" through an "imaginary committee." Nonetheless, they did not, as one critic charged, curb "a spontaneous expression of purpose of millions of American veterans." Instead, the Legion's founders channeled a set of beliefs common to servicemen of all ranks into one organization. The Legion directed the average soldier into an organization that combined the ideals for which he had fought with his concerns about the present and future. The Legion's leaders didn't conceal their feelings—they hated "slackers" and "Reds"; eagerly cooperated with local, state, and national authorities; established friendly relations with the business community; and lobbied for the special needs of veterans. These were part of the "Americanism" that became the Legionnaires' creed. Some ex-servicemen may have joined simply to renew acquaintances or enhance benefits. But the Legion provoked enough controversy for veterans themselves to judge the organization. It says a good deal for the Legion that even had every officer in the AEF joined the Legion in its first year, three-quarters of its members would still have been former enlisted personnel.

Thus, the Legion reached its embryonic stage. The morale conference lasted three days, and the issue was soon forgotten, though the Legion was aided when its future leaders persuaded Pershing that his army no longer required a full-time drill regimen. Pershing also released and adhered to a demobilization schedule whereby men stationed in Europe could anticipate a definite departure date. After discussions continuing until midnight on the final day, the Committee of Twenty made two important decisions. The new organization would begin in France, rather than waiting until all servicemen were home. A Paris caucus, to be held March 15–17, 1919, would initiate it. The rationale was "to establish the tradition of having the organization formed in France, the scene of America's bitterest tragedies and glorious victories," wrote Lieutenant Colonel George A. White, an Oregonian who became secretary of the Executive Committee elected at the Paris Caucus. Timing and location were consequently determining factors in the decision.

Another reason for the quick beginning was that competing veterans' groups, some with radical and pro-Bolshevik sympathies, were springing up on both sides of the Atlantic. This certainly had its impact upon Colonel Roosevelt and others at the Paris Caucus. The most dangerous rival that the fledgling American Legion faced was a loosely organized group initially known as the Private Soldiers and Sailors Legion and later titled the World War Veterans. Under a leadership that claimed to have been in uniform during the war, the group drafted a "declaration of principles and constitution" that circulated nationwide in early 1919. Whereas the American Legion wanted to unify and heal divisions in American society, the World War Veterans called for radicalism and class warfare. The radicals demanded that the federal government prosecute "incompetent and unfair officers" who had subjected "thousands of soldiers . . . to needless hardships and privations" in courts-martial for "petty infringements of military discipline." They further insisted that Congress provide employment for all veterans and a $500 (as opposed to a $60) discharge bonus. These groups and individuals clearly wanted to exploit the discontent among veterans and civilians about an unsettled economy. Openly pro-Soviet, the World War Veterans later denounced the American Legion as "a tool of monopoly and privilege."

The most urgent task was to sell the American Legion to the veteran. Lieutenant Colonels Wood, White, and Ralph D. Cole of Ohio (who served with the 37th Division) were named to a "committee of three" to get the movement started, Colonel D'Olier recalled. He added that Cole had to drop out after the February 16 meeting "while Wood, by his untiring energy and initiative, did the really big piece of work in getting the Paris Caucus together."

Getting the message to the doughboy was Wood's primary responsibility. He had to get all divisions to send delegates to the gathering. With the caucus only a month away, the manner and speed of communications was critical. Legwork was the only way to contact all officers and enlisted men, which was essential for a viable and enduring organization. Wood also had to get the foreign press to attend. Public relations as such was just coming into its own, and Colonel Wood did the pioneer work in a field that has been given strong emphasis by the Legion since its inception. Colonel White also worked among the various divisions. In a Dodge bearing "GHQ" license plates, he drove through France, Luxembourg, and occupied Germany, visiting combat units and urging them to send delegates to the caucus. Colonel D'Olier made similar visits to supply and service units. Others from the Committee of Twenty secured accommodations for delegates and reserved the Cirque de Paris for the site of the meeting.

The early organizers first encountered skepticism among potential members. Colonel White said, "Having started out with such decent motives and altruistic intentions, some of us were unprepared for the atmosphere of suspicion that came with the call for the Paris Caucus and the embryonic American Legion." A few contended that the proposed organization was simply a scheme to elect "Black Jack" Pershing to the presidency in 1920. Ironically, Pershing was involved with a competing veterans' organization, Comrades in Service, that had been supported for a time by President Wilson. Other critics repeated the already familiar charge that the American Legion was a plot by the general staff to manipulate AEF members into supporting universal military training. As Wood recalled in his later years, the reverse occurred: "General Headquarters opposed the Legion until it picked up so much steam that it ran over General Headquarters."

More than a few voiced the suspicion that the new organization was designed to promote Colonel Roosevelt's political career. To end these rumors, White and Wood asked Bennett C. Clark to preside at the caucus. Colonel Roosevelt was from a prominent Republican family, while "Champ" Clark had strong Democratic ties. With both involved in the Legion, it could hardly be characterized as a purely political effort. Also, suspicions persisted that the organization was merely the creation of a clique of officers, so equal representation was granted to enlisted men on the 100-member Executive Committee elected at the caucus.

The caucus met on schedule at the Cirque de Paris. As temporary chairman, Wood furiously sent out messages trying to raise attendance. Vincent A. Carroll, a Pennsylvanian who later was a member of the state Legion's recruiting committee, brought thirty men from the 77th Division. Still, despite the best efforts of Wood and others, officers outnumbered enlisted men about nine to one among the eventual 450 registrants. No Navy man appeared until the last day, when two sailors, according to Wood, "were kidnapped off the sidewalk" and another attended in the hope of seeing a show. Many enlisted men who had signed up were distracted by the amusements of Paris. Even the officers were greatly tempted; only 230 disciplined delegates "stuck it out and stayed off Paris." Still, *Stars and Stripes* described the caucus as a "broadly representative group." It also emphasized the speeches and motions made by enlisted men as demonstrations of the "true democracy of the Paris Caucus."

Actually, the small attendance and officer majority benefited Legion organizers. Guided by the founding circle of Wood, D'Olier, and White, the caucus planned how the group would be organized in the United States. It called for a veterans' caucus to be held in St. Louis for those "who had returned to America and [the] many troops [who] were denied the great privilege of coming to France to fight the Germans." Debate was strictly limited to a five-minute speech per delegate on each topic, setting a precedent for Legion conventions according to the procedure in the U.S. House of Representatives. The caucus didn't commit the organization on such issues as membership in the League of Nations, so from its inception, the Legion established neutrality on matters that might severely divide veterans.

Though only five paragraphs long, the temporary constitution that the caucus drafted aided the Legion immeasurably. It extended membership to all veterans of 1917–18, whether they had served overseas or not. This gave the Legion twice the potential membership of the Veterans of Foreign Wars, which was limited to men in a combat theater. The caucus also stipulated that each state unit of the eventual American Legion could handle all internal matters "except that the requirements and purposes of the national consitution shall be complied with." By endorsing this autonomy, the Legion sidestepped potential controversies and permitted each state to emphasize what it thought most appropriate. Finally, to affirm "Americanism" and define it in the most comprehensive and understandable way, the caucus adopted a provisional preamble extensively borrowed from that of the Grand Army of the Republic:

> We, the members of the military and naval reserves of the United States of America in the Great War, desiring to perpetuate the principles of justice, freedom, and democracy for which we have fought, to inculcate the duty and obligation of the citizen to the state, to preserve the history and incidents of our participation in the war, and to cement the ties of our comradeship formed in service, do propose to found and establish an association for the furtherance of the foregoing purposes.

The caucus gave the organization a name as well as a constitution. Several were suggested—Army of the Great War, Comrades of the Great War, Society of the Great War, American Comrades of the Great War, Great Legion, or simply, the Legion. Others considered at the caucus and in the United States included American Crusaders and even the Grand Army of the World. The provisional committee on choosing a name preferred Legion of the Great War but the caucus overruled it. Memories of the earlier American Legion created by the Plattsburghers and by Americans who served in the Canadian army before 1917 determined the final choice. The designation "American Legion" thus permitted even men who had not left basic training to identify with those who had served in France.

When the caucus adjourned, most of the more prominent delegates returned to join Theodore Roosevelt Jr.'s stateside recruiting drive. Wood again played a pivotal role. He sent telegrams to every state, seeking out men who were representative of veterans there. He also contacted the heads of more established veterans' groups, urging them to join the Legion in order to unite for the interests of the veteran. To rebut allegations that officers controlled the Legion, he prominently displayed the names of local enlisted men in promotional materials. On April 10, 1919, Wood advised every governor of the Legion's patriotic, non-partisan nature and urged them to "take an active interest in the formation." Roosevelt and Wood sent follow-up telegrams asking all who accepted the invitations to arrange state veterans' caucuses and local publicity for the campaign. Later that month, the 100-member Executive Committee was elected to administer affairs until the St. Louis Caucus, scheduled for May 8–10, 1919, and then until the first national convention in Minneapolis on November 10–12, 1919—the first anniversary of the World War armistice.

Compared with the meeting in Paris, the St. Louis Caucus was far more open to input from enlisted men and veterans at large. It was left to state units—usually the politicians or veterans originally contacted by Wood—to pick delegates. To circumvent any disputes over credentials, caucus chairman Henry Lindsley and the Executive Committee allowed each delegation twice as many votes as its state had members in the House of Representatives. This made attendance at the St. Louis Caucus more "democratic" and balanced than the gathering in Paris. Officers still accounted for more than half of the delegates, but the larger number of enlisted men than in Paris enabled Legion publicists to present it as a place where "rank counted for nothing," according to D'Olier.

The St. Louis Caucus met for a number of purposes. Organizers wanted to present the Legion in the most positive light; it was no accident that a disproportionate number of the delegates were publishers, editors, or reporters. Furthermore, they prepared very general statements—resolutions against radicalism or a vague endorsement for veterans' benefits—that could not be considered controversial. Finally, the give-and-take debate in the opening two days gave the Legion the appearance and substance of grass-roots democracy. Dorothy Harper, the historian of the Hawaii Department of the American Legion, noted, "The St. Louis Caucus was one of rip, roar, and tear, as every man pawed the earth to make himself heard and get his ideas over." Still, the caucus passeed resolutions asking for "the United States Congress to pass a bill deporting every one of those Bolsheviks or IWWs." The "IWWs" or "Wobblies," as they were known, had taken an anti-war stance and were widely suspected of engaging in sabotage and organizing strikes. They later engaged in a bloody clash with Legionnaires at Centralia, Washington, in which five veterans, four Legionnaires, and one Wobbly were killed. Other resolutions dealt with unemployment among veterans, medical care for the sick and disabled, and protection of veterans' widows and orphans.

The St. Louis Caucus bypassed matters that might have divided veterans. The Bonus, or as its proponents termed it, "adjusted compensation," was the biggest issue. Many veterans believed that they deserved a cash award of $15 to $30 per month of military service, since many patriotic men, according to one Pennsylvania delegate, "left lucrative employment upon joining the colors . . . at a time when many of the aliens [who] remained in safety at home were enjoying the advantage of an exceptionally high war wage." Eric Fisher Wood later noted that soon after the end of the war "every political demagogue" in the country got involved in the issue. Some fifty-five bonus schemes were introduced in Congress, ranging from a direct cash allotment to combinations of farm-and-home purchase assistance, land re-settlement, and even a proposal for vocational training. By the end of the year, it was left to the American Legion to sort out the best, and most practical, solution to the dilemma.

Apart from taking stands on veterans' benefits and Bolshevism, the St. Louis Caucus organized the framework that would help the Legion grow quickly in the next year. The Legion's declaration of principles, which eventually became the constitution's preamble, was soon written by Hamilton Fish of New York. The temporary constitution provided for the Executive Committee (two members from each state and the District of Columbia) and a full-time chairman and secretary. The committee authorized the state caucuses to organize "departments" that chartered local "posts." A public relations committee was assembled; it offered a prize for the design of a Legion emblem. The committee also hired Ivy Lee, who before the war headed the successful publicity drive for the Red Cross, to organize an advertising campaign. Thus, within a few days, the foundation of the American Legion had been laid.

Wood said the St. Louis Caucus united veterans of all ethnic groups, classes, and regions. The Executive Committee eventually delegated a group of spokesmen, including D'Olier and Wood, to devote their full energies to recruiting. Between the caucus and the November convention in Minneapolis, the Legion's "kingmakers," as they jokingly referred to themselves later, spoke often to business groups, reunions of AEF units, and civic organizations. Between June and November 1919, they criss-crossed the nation, conveying the message that the Legion not only represented veterans but, as Wood later wrote, that in a country besieged "by worldwide social and economic displacements, the American Legion will be the greatest bulwark against Bolshevism and anarchy." From the start, the Legion viewed its cause as that of the nation at large.

By August, organizers were convinced they had made great strides. Wood considered the drive to be "80 to 90 percent successful." Among them, Wood, D'Olier, and Theodore Roosevelt Jr. toured more than forty states. In September, the Legion was granted a national charter by Congress, which it had never done for previous veterans' organizations. In the same month, new posts elected delegates to state conventions scheduled in October, a month before the national convention. The state conventions usually adopted proposals suggested by the Legion's organizers. Wood concluded: "To have done the work outside of the above schedule would in the long run have caused a loss of valuable time, and in addition would probably have given the Legion such a reputation for inefficiency and have caused so many needless confusions, that it might have ruined our prospects of success."

In the crucial year of 1919, the nation's press, politicians, and government endorsed the Legion's cause. *The New York Herald,* the *Philadelphia Inquirer,* the *Pittsburgh Gazette,* and the *Los Angeles Express,* among others, opened themselves to Legion publicists and gave the organization unqualified support. A Pittsburgh newspaper editorialized:

> The more that is heard of the plans and personnel of the American Legion . . . the more general the popular approval. . . . One feature that stands out is its sturdy democracy. . . . The differences that were necessary, and so recognized during the period of active service, were promptly cast aside when the brave men met in civilian life.

At the Minneapolis convention, the leadership expressed its "most deep appreciation and loyal thanks to the press and all papers, magazines, and publicity committees who have so generously assisted the American Legion." Elected officials played a significant role, too. The governors of quite a few states, including New Jersey and Ohio, headed their states' preliminary organizations. As early as August 1919, the War Department gave the Legion "official recognition and assistance." The federal agency allowed the Legion to help potential Legionnaires obtain federal benefits for veterans, and even issued guns to Legion posts for ceremonial purposes.

In the midst of the Red Scare of 1919, the Legion was quickly welcomed by local and state officials. As one Legion organizer noted, "When the Legion officials needed anything, they called on the governor . . . the attorney general, and they got what they wanted right on the spot. There was no unnecessary red tape or correspondence, there were no letters to get into the hands of a secretary or a stenographer, because the Legion secretary would go direct to whoever he wished to see and get results pronto."

In Pennsylvania, county committees were organized under
the supervision of Carroll, Billy Murdock of Northumberland
County, and former Colonel Frank Thompson of the 28th Division. These committees enlisted support "from . . . the conservative foreign element of the large cities, the prominent Negroes,
and all the prominent business and professional people of the
state." Rather than simply appealing to veterans to sign up,
Legion committees sought out ex-servicemen who had not taken
advantage of the services available to them. The state organizing
committee then set up a section to aid the many unemployed
Pennsylvania veterans. By the end of the year, 50,000 Pennsylvania veterans had been hired by U.S. Steel alone. Local service
offices also gave meal vouchers to luckless veterans, kept lists of
veterans being cared for in local hospitals, and followed up on
the care given to the men. Legion organizers in Pennsylvania
were particularly sensitive to the problems of recruiting in large
cities like Pittsburgh and Philadelphia, where ethnic and neighborhood ties were often more important than past military service. In other cases, the Legion organized posts based upon
occupational associations. In Pittsburgh alone, posts were organized for advertising people, newspapermen, businessmen, and
machinists. By the end of the year, Pennsylvania had registered
117 posts, behind only Massachusetts (124) and New York
(130). Williamsport's Post #1 was the largest in the state, with
more than 850 members.

Despite moral support from many quarters, the Legion
received little financial aid. By early summer 1919, "not one single contribution had been received," and a frantic Eric Fisher
Wood even stated that "the situation has reached a point where
serious consideration should be given to the advisability of cur-
tailing or even completely closing the national office." To meet
early expenses, affluent members of the Executive Committee,
including Wood and D'Olier, lent the Legion $5,000 each. To
cover operating expenses from June to November, the Legion
eventually obtained loans of $250,000 from prominent banks
and wealthy individuals. New York's Morgan Guaranty Trust put
up most of the money; some wealthy Legionnaires guaranteed
the loan. When news of the Morgan loan became public, critics
called the money proof of the Legion's dependence on Wall Street
and the capitalist class. If so, Wall Street bankers did not bend

over backward to help the Legion; it had to pay back the money in five years at 6 percent interest. Indeed, the Legion quickly became antagonistic toward big business. In two of its biggest legislative fights of the interwar period, over the Bonus and for veterans' benefits, the Legion was usually at odds with economy-minded business groups such as the National Chamber of Commerce and the National Association of Manufacturers.

In constructing a national constituency, Legion organizers carefully stayed out of "politics" in the strictly partisan sense, avoiding the example of the GAR, with its exclusive Republican ties. Again, to avoid the appearance of partisanship, Theodore Roosevelt Jr. played no major role in Legion affairs after 1919. By 1920, the founders had declared that candidates for political office could not be officers in the Legion. Legion spokesmen would thus be promoting the organization or veterans' causes first and not be consumed with building their political careers. As Wood phrased it in a Legion newspaper, once the organization was formed, it was the moment "to let the rank and file who had not been G—d—d colonels run the Legion, as was their right."

The November convention still had to decide on substantive matters, such as the election of a national commander, the establishment of a permanent national headquarters, and an official stand on the Bonus. Franklin D'Olier, who had served stateside in the supply corps during the war, was chosen by the Legion's "kingmakers" to appeal to members who had been abroad. After a flurry of debate, he won overwhelmingly. Neither Washington (a hotbed of "corruption and rottenness," according to one Legionnaire) nor Chicago (run by the "Pro-Bolshevik German Burgomeister" William Hale Thompson) were considered suitable sites for a permanent headquarters. Some intensive lobbying on behalf of Indianapolis eventually succeeded, and it was chosen on the second ballot by a vote of 361 to 323.

The most immediate issue at the convention was the amount of annual dues. The Executive Committee insisted that without a well-funded newspaper, the new *American Legion Weekly*, members wouldn't know what the Legion stood for and the group would "lapse into disconnected, disjointed, uncoordinated groups of posts." The first issue of the *Weekly*, published July 4, 1919, was intended to entertain and inform the Legionnaire—and the public—of the activities of the organization and its perspective on issues. The funding of such a publication would require dues of at least four times the 25-cent level established at the St. Louis Caucus. Delegates from states with large memberships, such as Pennsylvania, said the steep increase would reduce membership and shut out poor veterans. But after two stormy roll-call votes and some maneuvering by Wood, national dues of $1 were approved 384 to 300.

A more intractable problem was the dispute over "adjusted compensation," or the Bonus. Some members argued that there could be "no price for patriotism" and feared that the immediate payment of a bonus would unleash a ruinous inflation. The main figures on the Executive Committee—Wood, Roosevelt, and D'Olier—wished to avoid a firm stand for fear of losing members. To Bonus advocates, however, avoiding a stand was interpreted as subtle opposition to the measure. In Minneapolis, the Legion ultimately endorsed adjusted compensation in theory without offering any specific means of financing it, thus reversing the decision at the St. Louis Caucus. Whether its leaders wanted it or not, the Legion was being forced into the front ranks of the Bonus struggle.

In its first year, the American Legion took great strides. It never attained the lofty expectations that "very shortly no man who wants to have it known and who is proud of having been in service will go on the streets without a Legion button on," but given the challenges it faced, it attained a level of success unknown to previous veterans' organizations. By slowly endorsing the Bonus and sidestepping issues such as the League of Nations, the Legion attained a greater national presence in the long run. Recruiting and remaining relevant to the issues of the time were challenges for both the national organization and state departments like Pennsylvania. That both succeeded in the ensuing years was a testament to the leaders and the rank and file. They united behind a comprehensive vision of "100 percent Americanism" that guided their policies and goals.

THE PENNSYLVANIA DEPARTMENT OF THE AMERICAN LEGION

The First Decade, 1919–28

The Department of Pennsylvania was founded on June 12, 1919, when the temporary national headquarters in New York granted it a charter. That is much like stating that a ship comes into existence on the date of its launching—much time, material, and effort are required to make it a going concern. The department's immediate origins, of course, go back to the historic meetings in Paris, where several Pennsylvanians played important parts in helping launch the national organization. Second Lieutenant George H. Tyler opened a headquarters in Philadelphia to organize the American Legion on April 6, 1919. He was assisted by William Gulliam Aertsen Jr., who acted as secretary, and Edward Baird, who was the department's first finance officer. Later that year, National Commander D'Olier, fresh from his election at the Minneapolis convention, congratulated Tyler and his fellow department officers by noting "that in no other state in the union has there been put over a more substantial job than in the state of Pennsylvania."

Early Pennsylvania Legion posts were as diverse as the state itself. The first to be chartered was the Garrett Cochrane Post #1 of Williamsport, on June 10, 1919. Soon, this was the largest post in the state, with more than 850 members. Philadelphia's Post #297 gained new members at a rate of thirty-five per week after its initial organizing drive in the summer of 1919. It had the distinction of having members in active service in the army of occupation in Germany. Dehaven Hinkson, an African-American doctor who served in a field hospital in France, returned to West Philadelphia to help organize the George I. Cornish Post #292. He was awarded the American Legion's Distinguished Service Medal in 1969. By the end of 1919, 60,801 former soldiers, sailors, and Marines were enlisted in the Pennsylvania department.

How well did this nucleus work? Pennsylvania had the largest delegation at the St. Louis Caucus in May 1919. The emerging leadership of the Pennsylvania department worked closely with the national office in New York to ensure the widest representation of delegates. The future national commander, Franklin D'Olier, advised Tyler to add three delegates—all from organized labor—to the temporary state committee. These veterans—Lieutenant Joseph Fraye, Private Paul Jones of Scranton, and Lieutenant Bernard J. Voll of Philadelphia—proved that the state Legion was not restricted to a certain social element. Provisions also were made for the inclusion of injured and disabled veterans. County organizations were instructed to make every effort to have as many men present at these meetings as possible. Tyler reminded D'Olier (also registered as a delegate from Pennsylvania) that it was "of the utmost importance that the entire Pennsylvania delegation should travel together in order that representatives of committees, etc., may be elected and a definite program evolved for the work of the delegation." By early October 1919, the department had registered 38,000 members and received 200 identification certificates for delegates to the Minneapolis convention. Even before the convention, Pennsylvanians were quick to realize their

strength. On October 6, 1919, Tyler asked D'Olier to deal with
an issue:

> It is extremely important that at this time the Pennsylva-
> nia delegation is seated either on the stage or else in front
> of the convention hall. You will recall that at St. Louis,
> the Pennsylvania delegation was seated in the extreme
> rear and being the delegation of the second-largest state
> in the union, there is a very bitter feeling about it. . . .
> Many delegates from this state indeed have felt that the
> national headquarters being located in New York laid
> itself open to much criticism in seating the second-
> largest delegation in such an inconspicuous place.

The first national convention, held in Minneapolis in November 1919, honored Pennsylvania by selecting D'Olier to serve
the one-year term of national commander. This did not take
place without a spirited debate. Some delegates were opposed to
a national commander who had served stateside in the supply
corps. Hamilton Fish of New York led the opposition and put for-
ward Iowa's Hanford MacNider, noting his nine combat decorations and his origins west of the Mississippi, far from the New
York office that had run the organization from the start. Another
candidate, Emmett O'Neal of Kentucky, was nominated for
much the same reason. D'Olier won overwhelmingly, in part
because the opposition was disorganized. The Legion's founders
retained control of the organization for one more year and Pennsylvania didn't have another national commander until Paul
Griffith was elected at the 1946 national convention.

From the start, the American Legion became the most visible
proponent of the rights and entitlements of veterans. The problems of returning veterans were widely recognized. Some businesses gave them back their previous jobs. "Pennsylvania's war
heroes will find a welcome from former employers and a guarantee of work," said the magazine *North America*. The article
noted that Pennsylvania Railroad re-employed more than
19,000 returning servicemen in the first six months after demobilization. Other employers were not nearly as eager to do so.
W.A. Kelton, the business representative of the International
Association of Machinists, charged that certain employers

refused to rehire veterans and kept their wartime replacements because many jobs were filled by women who accepted lower wages. The special problems of the disabled also needed to be addressed. A representative from the state Department of Labor and Industry noted, "The government has failed to plan properly for the big reconstruction problem. . . . The states must stop scrapping the valuable economic manpower represented in the handicapped man." The Pennsylvania Legion department's most pressing tasks were the re-employment of veterans and their assimilation back into American society.

The Legion's organization proceeded rapidly in Pennsylvania. The first statewide meeting of Legionnaires was in Harrisburg on October 2–4, 1919. The fledgling organization had to organize the county caucuses to elect the 200 delegates to be sent to the Minneapolis convention. William G. Murdock presided, and Tyler was elected department commander. Elected as vice commanders were Alexander Vaughn, Lyell Spangler, and Harry C. Blank. The Rev. Joseph L.N. Wolfe was elected department chaplain and Margaret C. Thomas was named historian. Tyler appointed William G. Aertsen as department adjutant and Edgar W. Baird as finance officer. All officers were designated as temporary until the national convention met the next month.

Controversy over the role of Legion posts in local labor disputes troubled the organization from the start. On the first day of the meeting, delegates adopted a statement saying "that the American Legion has no participation in disputes between labor and capital but that it stands unalterably for the preservation of law and order." The relationship between trade unions and the Legion was troublesome in the early years. Individual posts across the nation helped to break certain strikes that were deemed as either disruptive or led by Bolsheviks. In the steel towns of western Pennsylvania and in Pittsburgh, Legion members escorted replacement workers to their jobs. In some cases, veterans just released from service took the places of the strikers. Other Pennsylvania Legionnaires quickly defended unionist members. In a letter to the *American Legion Weekly*, Robert F. Jones of Philadelphia, a member of the Lawrence Delaney Post #26 who belonged to a local boilermakers' union, urged all union men in the Legion to "be on their guard against any objectionable strikebreaking activities cropping out in local posts." He noted that many union locals worked hard for veterans and tried to solve their problems in the workplace. Philadelphia's Steamfitters Local #331 worked with officials at the Hog Island shipyard on "giving better positions and higher pay to disabled soldiers." This local and others like it, Jones cautioned, were not filled with Bolsheviks.

The department met formally in convention in Allentown in June 1920 and accomplished a good deal under Eric Fisher Wood, who presided as chairman. A permanent constitution was adopted and the Women's Auxiliary was established. To ensure proper representation for all Legionnaires, the new constitution provided for three vice chairmen, one each from the eastern, central, and western parts of the state. The boundaries for the three sections were those of the caucus districts that had been formed at the first convention to facilitate communication among Legionnaires. The department also endorsed the principle (adopted earlier by the national organization) of refusing to formally discuss or take action on international issues unless "a primary American interest was involved." The following department officers were chosen for 1920–21: David J. Davis, commander; David Simpson of Philadelphia, eastern vice commander; C.C. McLain of Indiana, western vice commander; and M.E. Finney of Harrisburg, central vice commander. "Billy" Murdock of Milton was eventually selected as adjutant. Davis of Scranton, a former chief of staff of the 26th ("Keystone") Division, was selected over several others, including Colonel Frank H. Thompson of the division's 110th Infantry and Murdock, who had been prominent in the Pennsylvania Selective Service system. Finally, Wolfe was named department chaplain and Tyler became the national executive committeeman.

The 1920 convention also was the birthplace of a distinct Legion organization whose very existence promoted the national group. Former Major Joseph W. Breen of Philadelphia, a participant in the Paris Caucus, proposed a "side order" within the Legion that would promote community service and "keep alive the more humorous incidents of our service." Breen seems to have raised the idea in 1920 at a meeting of about twenty members of the Breen-McCracken Post in West Philadelphia.

William L. Charr, a friend of Breen who was at the meeting, said Breen even had a name picked out.

The same year, the Pennsylvania department recognized "La Societe des 40 Hommes et 8 Chevaux" at its Allentown convention. The society's name, a reference to the type of French railroad car capable of carrying forty men and eight horses that was used to transport soldiers across the Western Front, conjured up wartime experiences and the camaraderie felt by those who served overseas. To become a "voyageur" (the society's locals were termed "voitures"), a Legionnaire must have been a standout in post activities. The post then nominated him for the "funmaking society." In a short time, this "playground of the Legion," as it was termed by many, ran a child welfare program and took orphans and underprivileged children to ball games and circuses and on picnics. The "Forty and Eight" grew to national prominence as other state Legions imitated the Pennsylvania model. In 1921, it was accepted by the national organization at its convention in Cleveland. Soon, "Forty and Eight" parades and pranks became a regular—and controversial—feature of Legion conventions. The "Forty and Eight" often organized mock train wrecks at conventions, in which hotel property and other businesses were sometimes damaged. Official Legion statements usually denied any responsibility for the activities of the group. After an incident at the 1941 convention in Milwaukee, the "Forty and Eight" leader claimed that his group was "as usual, sacrificing itself for the Legion. . . . We are glad to do the drinking for the Legion; we are glad to go to jail for the Legion; we will do anything for the Legion."

The next convention was held in Pittsburgh in September 1921. Several candidates emerged for the position of department commander for 1921–22, and Joseph H. Thompson of Beaver Falls was selected. Francis A. Lewis of Philadelphia was named eastern vice commander, Lucius M. Crumrine of Washington was elected western vice commander, and Mark Milnor of Harrisburg was named central vice commander. Murdock was retained as department adjutant, and membership was 58,113.

The year 1921 was marked by a surge of activity by the Legion on behalf of sick and disabled veterans. More than 11,300 cases were taken up by the Veterans Bureau through the regional agencies of the State Committee on Medical Aid and

behalf he labored tirelessly." He was a delegate to the Allentown, Pittsburgh, Williamsport, and Reading conventions. On December 1, 1923, he rose to department adjutant.

Deighan continued the success of past administrations. He offered an example to district deputy commanders to keep them building membership. He "was on duty at his desk early and late, replying to each of the almost 11,700 communications" he received during his first term in office, "in almost every case on the same day it was received," according to one Harrisburg Legionnaire. Deighan coordinated the annual recruiting drives, in which he worked closely with the department commander. Even with a greatly reduced office staff, "he managed so skillfully that records and other office routine were kept up to date at all times."

Under Collins and Deighan, the state legion ventured into new areas in 1924. A permanent committee was established to arrange and supervise Legion radio programming in the state. "Knowing full well" that initial attempts to put together a program would "prove somewhat crude" (as the *Legion Annual* put it), a plan was coordinated by the local chairmen in Pittsburgh, Scranton, Harrisburg, Altoona, and Philadelphia who believed that radio would ultimately prove the best way to promote the Legion. In Philadelphia, a Legion program combining "patriotism and entertainment" was followed by more than 1,000 inquiries about membership. In Pittsburgh, the initial program was a broadcast of a banquet for Collins. Glendon T. Tongue, chairman of the Radio Committee, "sat in his home in Philadelphia, some 300 miles away, and heard every word plainly," according to the *Legion Annual.*

Legion posts in other towns and cities put on their own radio shows. Scranton presented a program on the Bonus. Altoona broadcast all-Legion talent nights, to stimulate membership drives throughout the area. Finally, Philadelphia's Tioga Post #319 performed the first Legion "radio ritual" when it made Harry E. Erhart, known as the city's "Dream Daddy" of musical entertainment and director of station WDAR, a member. This also sparked inquiries about Legion membership.

From August 21–23, 1924, the state convention was held in Greensburg. J. Mitchell Chase of Clearfield was overwhelmingly elected department commander. Earl A. Ziegenfus of Bethlehem was eastern vice commander, Dr. Joseph J. Bellas of Lansford was central vice commander, and Henry S. Coshey Jr. of Greensburg was western vice commander. The Rev. William K. Newton of Honesdale was named department chaplain. The new commander retained Deighan as adjutant for another year. John F. Dervin was re-elected by the Executive Committee as finance officer.

Frankford Post #211 was the second-largest in Philadelphia and the tenth-largest in the state. It and other posts in the Philadelphia area employed a "flying squadron" of delinquent dues collectors. This group hopped into automobiles and made unannounced calls (usually on Sundays) on those who were in arrears. Such tactics helped the post claim 550 paid-up members by 1924.

The Frankford post maintained a home that the *Philadelphia Inquirer* called "one of the most up to date, having within it all the comforts of a real home." Furnishings included a lending library of more than 1,600 volumes, a game room, a ladies' and board room, and two parlors with radio sets. By becoming a community center for the Kiwanis or Rotary Clubs, as well as a meeting place for veterans, the Frankford post built a relationship with civic organizations that increased exposure and membership for the Legion by sponsoring dinners, entertainment, and fund-raising activities. By 1925, the post home was turning a monthly profit of $200.

Veterans' matters, however, remained the primary concern. From its inception, the post maintained a caisson for funerals as well as twelve rifles and an honor guard. In 1921, the post had full charge of fifty-seven military funerals and provided an escort, firing squad, and grave marker for each veteran. The post also delved into bread-and-butter issues. Its employment officer found jobs for ninety-eight veterans in 1920 and 130 in 1921. Disabled veterans also received attention, with the post's "lawyer comrades" giving legal aid free or at a nominal charge. Every Wednesday after 1924, a post committee rendered, according to a post newsletter, "full assistance without one cent of charge to veterans or their dependents" in their attempts to obtain the Bonus from Washington.

Post #211 maintained a constant public profile by its civic involvement. Every year members assisted in a popular picnic called the Lawn Festival of the Frankford Hospital. The Frankford Athletic Association received the post's financing and support for the Frankford Yellow Jackets football club, later to be the Philadelphia Eagles. In turn, the south stand at the Yellow Jacket stadium was known as the Legion Stand, where Legionnaires and their friends rooted the team on.

The Frankford post constantly sought to involve veterans in activities. It maintained a baseball team, a track club, pool and billiard rooms, and swimming programs for members and their dependents. In 1923, the post sponsored Boy Scout Troop #211. A twelve-piece post orchestra played at picnics and other community events, and card parties were regular events.

Perhaps the most notable asset of the Frankford post was its prize-winning Drum and Bugle Corps. It began in March 1922, when Harry Whiteling and two other Legionnaires persuaded the post that a corps would benefit veterans and the community. On April 6, 1922, the corps had its first practice with ten members, though only one bugler and one drummer had any experience. Even the drums were on loan from the Spanish War Veterans. The auxiliary later purchased drums for the corps and the band purchased a standard bugle for every man. The corps wore regulation Army and Navy uniforms. It quickly grew and its first public appearance was during a parade at the opening of the new Yellow Jackets stadium on November 10, 1922. The corps eventually numbered more than fifty. On February 22, 1924, the group captured first prize at the annual ball of the Philadelphia County American Legion against what was called the strongest competition in the city. In Greensburg on August 23, 1924, the corps took the first prize of $200 in the competition at the annual state Legion convention. That year, at the national convention in San Antonio, Texas, the Frankford post corps won third place in the national competition.

Another that made its mark was the Helen Fairchild Nurses Post of Philadelphia. It was named for a Pennsylvania nurse who was attached to Base Hospital #10 and died during unspecified action on the front in France on January 18, 1918. The post was organized on October 4, 1919, at the Frankford Hospital. Later meetings were held at hospitals throughout the city and eventually, through the efforts of the director of the Third Street Armory, the post found permanent headquarters there. In 1934, it moved to the Central Y.M.C.A. at 1412 Arch Street.

The Fairchild post's membership, representing virtually all the hospitals in the Philadelphia area, was in fact from across the United States and several foreign countries. Two of its members had received the Distinguished Service Cross; one was wounded during the AEF retreat from Amiens, France. Its membership was fairly constant. In 1919, it was 200; in 1926, it peaked at 386. This temporary increase was shared by other posts because the costs of the overseas trip made it necessary to pay two years of dues to be eligible for the convention in Paris in 1927.

The post was well represented at all state and national conventions. During its early years, one or two members were always chosen for the color guard of the department delegation. Later, eight or ten members were chosen by the commander to carry the red and white "Pennsylvania" banner. The post also claimed to be the first in the state to grant the school award to girls. Members worked to extend this option to Legion posts throughout the state. They worked for this on the basis that "the Legion constitution admits of no class distinctions and that the government constitution declares women citizens." A motion introduced by the Fairchild post got this policy accepted department-wide at the fourth annual convention in 1923.

The convention in Erie from August 20–22, 1925, elected Lucius M. Crumrine of Washington as department commander; Jacob F. Miller of Somerton, eastern vice commander; Dr. E.J. Williams of Huntington, central vice commander; and Dr. C.A. Rodgers of Freeport, western vice commander. Legion activities were diverse in this year. The sale of poppies garnered more than $4,100 for welfare work. The commonwealth also took over the financing of the Legion service officers, James C. Purcell and George H. McGrath, by making them vocational administrators, greatly speeding up the clearing of cases brought up to regional offices in the Veterans Bureau. Finally, Vincent A. Carroll of Philadelphia was elected at the national convention in Omaha, Nebraska, as national vice commander.

The convention in Delaware Water Gap from September 9–11, 1926, elected as department commander Robert M. Vail of Kingston and also chose Daniel B. Stickler of Lancaster, Harry B. Bunting of Pittsburgh, and A.W. Sheasly of Emporium as vice commanders. Former department commander J. Leo Collins was elected national committeeman, with former Commander Lucius M. Crumrine as his alternate. The 1926 convention also changed the terms of department officers. Instead of running from the close of one department convention to the next, the new officers did not take their positions until the close of the 1926 national convention in Philadelphia and continued in office until the return of the Pennsylvania delegation from the Paris convention in the fall of 1927.

The long-anticipated national convention in Philadelphia coincided with the 150th anniversary of the signing of the Declaration of Independence. The Pennsylvania department claimed that the meeting "was staged on a scale never before attempted or equaled" and was "held in a tremendous auditorium." The Junior World Series was "played in the immense stadium" (Shibe Park) and viewed by Legionnaires from all states. More than 50,000 Legionnaires and auxiliary members participated in the convention parade, cheered on by hundreds of thousands of people along the route. The Navy dirigible *Los Angeles* and planes flew overhead, and the Colorado contingent loosed coyotes, mules, and other western animals along Broad Street. Pennsylvania, of course, had the largest delegation in the line, headed by its massed colors. To get a better view of festivities, Legionnaire Harry Gardiner of Johnstown climbed atop the statue of William Penn on City Hall.

More seriously, the national convention saw the emergence of new Legion personalities and policies. The convention honored Pennsylvania by selecting the Rev. Joseph L.N. Wolfe as national chaplain. Wolfe, a chaplain of the 28th Division, had previously been the first national chaplain of the "Forty and Eight." In addition, the Philadelphia convention determined that each post should assume some kind of community service annually. This was done to fulfill the pledge in the Legion's constitution "to inculcate a sense of individual obligation to the community, state, and nation."

The state convention in York from August 4–6, 1927, elected Edwin T. Hollenbeck of Philadelphia as department commander. It also chose Robert W. Neall of Lansdowne as eastern vice commander, Ray E. Taylor of Harrisburg as central vice commander, and Bernard L. Keenan of Johnsonburg as western vice commander. Rabbi Herman J. Beck of Pottsville was elected chaplain. James J. Deighan was retained for a fifth term as adjutant. The York convention ended, as the *Legion Annual* noted, with "all thoughts turning to the ninth national convention, to be held for the first time on foreign soil."

As in 1917, Pennsylvania in 1928 sent a large contingent to Paris to celebrate the tenth anniversary of America's entrance into the Great War. The trip to France on the Cunard steamships *Antonia* and *Tuscania* by the "second AEF" was heralded by its principal sponsor, Henry D. Lindsley of Texas, as "the greatest peaceful invasion in the history of the world." Pennsylvania had the largest delegation in Paris among the 2,100 Legionnaires; it was led by the lame-duck department Commander Robert Vail.

The convention opened with a formal meeting attended by the President of France and two heroes of the Great War, General John J. Pershing and Marshal Ferdinand Foch. A crowd of more than a million lined the streets from a point above the Arc de Triomphe to beyond the Cathedral of Notre Dame. Through this throng passed more than 20,000 Legionnaires from forty-eight states and several U.S. possessions and territories. Pennsylvania's delegation was led by the Legion band from Clearfield and the official Legion mascot, young Jay Ward, an orphan attending the Scotland School for children of soldiers and sailors who died in military service. Never before, according to several descriptions of the parade, had the Legion staged a finer procession or appeared against a more impressive background.

The parade was not merely part of a junket but was organized to commemorate the sacrifices of the Great War. The Legion was allowed to march in a body beneath the Arc de Triomphe, an honor usually reserved for victorious French armies. Legionnaires decorated the tomb of the unknown French soldier with flowers. After the procession, the tomb was covered with 20,000 personal floral tributes.

The former doughboys' mood created a carnival of comradeship. Many men broke through the crowds on the sidelines to greet marchers whom they recognized. One Pennsylvania Legionnaire had a note thrust into his hand, written in a childish script by a war orphan who expressed her thanks to "les Americains" who had recaptured her town. Many villages and small towns held celebrations of their own. Small groups of Legionnaires and auxiliary members "lost themselves in the pockmarked terrain around Verdun" or "went exploring in the sections around Reims," where there were "still many charred, broken tree stumps, white zigzag lines that mark the old trenches and acres of barbed wire." Many delegates visited at least one of the American Army cemeteries. In more than a few instances, they brought from home "little receptacles of earth, which they deposited with due reverence upon French soil, bringing back in exchange . . . earth from these perpetual American monuments in France," according to one Pennsylvania veteran. The Pennsylvania delegation also made official visits to surrounding countries. Tributes were placed upon tombs of the unknown soldier in Belgium, Britain, Italy, and Poland.

The Paris trip and convention culminated nearly a decade of Legion activity and service in Pennsylvania. The department had consistently maintained one of the highest memberships in the country, ranking second or third in the national organization. By the end of 1928, department membership was at 63,602. Pennsylvania led in a number of activities, notably Americanism and community service. The years ahead would present new challenges to both the leadership and rank and file of the Pennsylvania Legion.

CHAPTER

3

THE LEAN YEARS

*Pennsylvania Legionnaires
and the Great Depression,
1929–39*

The Paris convention ended the first decade of the American Legion. During that time, the Pennsylvania department passed its first test. A firm foundation was laid and upon it was an active and permanent body of more than 63,000 veterans. The years ahead saw more than a few challenges to this record, ones the Legion leadership worked hard to overcome.

Before the Depression, the most controversial event in the history of the Pennsylvania American Legion involved academic freedom and the Liberal Club at West Chester State Normal College. In April 1927, the trustees fired instructors Robert Kerlin and John Kinneman, who four years earlier had organized a campus chapter of the Liberal Club, a national organization that often criticized American foreign policy. After a meeting of the club at which the American intervention in Nicaragua was characterized as imperialistic, a coalition of local Legion posts questioned the "right of a tax-supported school to instill in the minds of future teachers a disrespect for the president of the United States," according to a department circular. The district's Americanism director soon investigated the club and criticized its connection with the American Civil Liberties Union, which supplied it with literature and speakers. This convinced certain members of the post that the club had been instigated by and was influenced by Communists. Kerlin and Kinneman, who had supported left-wing causes in the past, were subsequently fired. The Pennsylvania Legion Department and the school's trustees denied any connection between the two events, though the eastern vice commander applauded the efforts of the West Chester post against the "paid propaganda and the exaltation of doctrines which have as their purposes rendering America defenseless" and "accomplishing the destruction of the moral standards of students."

The denial by the West Chester and Philadelphia area posts was convincing to few—in and outside Pennsylvania. According to William Pencak's account of the incident in his *Study of the American Legion Between the World Wars,* the first protests about the incident "from the ACLU and their ilk," convinced the Legion that the professors were indeed "closet Communists." The *Philadelphia Inquirer* editorialized that "the prominence of the victims, the widespread publicity given to the cases . . . bid fair to make this a case about as famous as the Scopes trial." Even Hamilton Fish, the Legionnaire and conservative congressman from New York, deplored "such attacks by the American Legion or any other patriotic organization, which in the name of Americanism deprives American citizens from exercising their constitutional rights." Teachers at the college (not all of whom were Legion members) affirmed the firings, which were upheld in court. The case left a bad taste in many Pennsylvanians' mouths for years.

The Uniontown convention of August 23–25, 1928, elected Charles A. Gebert of Tamaqua as department commander for the coming year. Roy E. Sheetz was named eastern vice commander, with Harvey Bowman and Dr. Ralph B. McCord elected central and western vice commanders, respectively. Deighan continued as adjutant while Dervin was retained as finance officer.

Service to wounded and disabled veterans continued to be a primary mission of the Pennsylvania Legion. A cadre of trained and experienced service officers had been placed at the call of World War veterans throughout the state, regardless of Legion affiliation. One legionnaire said that this was "a sincere and willing group of Legionnaires, many of them professional men, who . . . served unselfishly and at considerable personal sacrifice." By the end of the decade, thousands of cases had been prepared, evidence located, and claims filed.

The Legion's role in the preservation of veterans' benefits was highlighted in local membership drives. One of the most valuable services provided by the local post, said J.A. Walker, commander of Post #305 in Wilkinsburg, was obtaining free hospitalization for all honorably discharged veterans, whether they were Legionnaires or not. "Hospital care for all sick veterans is but one of the benefit measures originated and passed through the backing of the Legion during its ten-year fight for the relief of veterans," added Dr. H.C. Scott, the post's service officer.

The struggle for veterans' benefits in Pennsylvania mirrored the fight to protect veterans under national policy. Veterans' benefits were controversial for some groups (particularly the American Medical Association) that intensely fought against the establishment of the Veterans Administration. The national Chamber of Commerce and later the self-styled National Economy League fought the Legion's legislative agenda on the ground that it would wreck the federal budget. Constant public relations work was used to put veterans' causes in the best possible light. There were moments, especially after the federal Economy Act of 1933 (which drastically cut veterans' benefits), when department representatives talked of breaking the "non-political" clause in the Legion charter and directly endorsing parties and candidates.

The American Legion's national legislative efforts attracted new members, and more than a few posts noted the favorable publicity gained for the organization. Post #305, designated the John M. Clark Post after a first officer from the 111th Infantry who was killed in action, assisted in admissions into the nearest veterans' hospitals. Frequently, the post was notified too late and the veteran's condition would not permit him to be moved.

This compounded the problem of the few facilities within the state. "The public is probably unaware of the crowded condition of many hospitals at this time," stated Dr. Scott in a local press briefing to the *Williamsburg Progress.*

The Pennsylvania Legion charged itself with putting the plight of the suffering and disabled on the front burner. Only after 1924, after considerable pressure from veterans' groups, was enough money allocated to build veterans' hospitals across the country. It was up to legislators from a given state, with prodding from the Legion, to lobby for adequate beds in their state.

Perhaps the most significant result was the construction of a Veterans Bureau hospital near Coatesville in 1930. About $2 million was allocated by the federal government for the completion of a psychiatric institution. The site was recommended after more than 130 locations were considered by Regional Director Harry J. Crosson, with the agreement of the Pennsylvania department. The facility was a group of buildings, from a recreation center for patients to housing for medical personnel. Eventually, the hospital, built on about 360 acres near the old Lincoln highway, could accommodate 1,200 patients.

Though services and benefits for the disabled were expanding, Pennsylvania facilities still were not up to the task. In a given year during the interwar period, the Veterans Bureau served thousands of patients, providing an average 51,250 medical examinations and more than 72,000 treatments. There was an average of 1,350 veterans in Pennsylvania hospitals at the end of every month between 1925 and 1939. This number was low in comparison with similar statistics for New York (3,100) and Illinois (2,100). Pennsylvania didn't have fewer disabled veterans; its veterans who required hospitalization were often sent out of state. This was a longstanding problem.

Much of this seemed to have been the result of benign or absolute neglect. In 1928, Edith Rogers, a congresswoman from Massachusetts and a long-time Legion supporter, sponsored a bill to appropriate $16 million for veterans' hospitals. However, there was no provision for new beds in Pennsylvania, arousing considerable anger among Keystone department officials and committees. They immediately surveyed the hospital facilities for Pennsylvania's disabled veterans and discovered that "conditions existed which were not only unwarranted but intolerable," according to the department commander. One condition was "an unfair discrimination" against Pennsylvania's disabled compared with those from other states, particularly New York and Illinois. Although Pennsylvania had given in service as many men as those states, New York had at home more than 80 percent of its tubercular veterans and Illinois more than 50 percent. Better than 93 percent of New York veterans designated as mental patients were cared for within that state, while Illinois provided for nearly 89 percent of them. Pennsylvania had but 36.5 percent of its mentally disabled at home. Of the 1,821 disabled veterans from the Keystone State in 1930, 832 were hospitalized at home, but 300 of them were not in veterans' hospitals but in the Naval Hospital at Philadelphia. The dispensary at Perry Point, Maryland, "warehoused" 543 of Pennsylvania's 989 mentally disabled veterans. Others were scattered from North Carolina to Arizona. The study also revealed that 380 mentally afflicted veterans "were being cared for and treated as paupers" in a number of private and public hospitals. The investigators concluded that "the disabled of Pennsylvania had been, either intentionally or otherwise, the objects of a vicious discrimination."

By 1930, the department focused its plea upon "a sufficient appropriation from Congress to provide additional hospitals in Pennsylvania so that all Pennsylvania veterans may be hospitalized in institutions in Pennsylvania," according to the Department's *Legion Annual.* Legislative requests by Pennsylvania congressmen, after consultation with the State Veterans' Commission, were for a diagnostic center in Philadelphia, the expansion of mental facilities in Coatesville, and the construction of a 500-bed tuberculosis hospital in north-central Pennsylvania. Unfortunately, economic constraints, especially the effects of the 1933 Economy Act, slowed the construction of veterans' facilities throughout the nation. Significant change would occur only after several years of hard effort.

Legion efforts did not end with the construction of hospitals. It aided rehabilitation efforts by finding new places for the disabled in society. Dr. Roger P. Hentz, acting medical officer at Philadelphia Veterans Hospital #49, lauded the Legion's poppy program. The organization raised funds for rehabilitation programs through the sale of poppies made by disabled veterans in

VA hospitals. "I believe," Hentz said at a Legion convention, "that the men enjoy making poppies more than any other occupational project undertaken. . . . It takes the men's minds away from their troubles, and too, they realize the purpose that the poppies serve." A physician at the Aspinwall hospital also noted the therapeutic effect: "It was always a pleasant sight to see these patients working on the poppies as their physical condition would allow. In making these poppies, the financial were not the only benefits derived . . . as the occupation of their hands and minds on light, pleasant work of this kind is always an advantage to the patient confined to his bed."

By the autumn of 1929, the economic tide that had swept Americans into a period of unrivaled prosperity abruptly shifted into the opposite direction. In October 1929, the Wall Street crash began the era known as the Great Depression. Soon, as many as one in five workers was unemployed. By the end of 1931, farm income had dropped to only half of what it had been in 1929. As conditions worsened, President Hoover continued to proclaim his confidence in the economy and insisted that "prosperity was just around the corner." All too quickly, veterans and others realized the desperate need for some relief, from any source.

In the early years of the Depression, the Pennsylvania Legion's first concern was to obtain immediate help for veterans. This was made even more pressing because of the usual problems of the sick and disabled. The American Legion under the direction of John F. Dervin also assisted the Veterans Bureau in other matters, notably the distribution of cash benefits to the guardians of 2,050 minors and of the 1,750 mentally incompetent veterans. Legion posts, with the help of the regional office of the Veterans Bureau, also served as clearinghouses for veterans' problems and issues. They distributed Bonus certificates and filed claims under the Emergency Officers' Retirement Act.

Earlier, in 1929, the Pennsylvania Legislature passed several measures sponsored by the American Legion, the most important of which was the establishment of the state Veterans' Commission. This agency surveyed and compiled data concerning veterans, recommended favorable legislation, advised the adjutant general, and handled pension and relief issues. The commission had five members, all of whom had to have served in the armed forces "while a state of war existed between the United States of America and another sovereign power," and be a member in good standing of a recognized veterans' organization in the state. Members received no compensation.

The new commission embarked on preserving and extending Legion contacts with state politicians. For example, the Scranton convention passed two resolutions urging the department's representatives to lobby hard to extend the "presumptive period" in mental and tubercular cases from 1925 to 1930. The presumptive period meant that veterans could apply for aid or rehabilitation until either 1925 or 1930 on the assumption that the malady was service-related. All veterans were presumed to have been in good health at the time of their inductions because they had received medical exams then to determine health status. Through the commission, Edwin T. Kelley and the Legislative Committee urged other veterans' groups to persuade the state's congressmen and senators to support the Rankin Bill, which would have extended the presumptive period and which was vetoed by President Hoover. Only one member of Pennsylvania's delegation opposed it. Eighteen other departments passed similar resolutions, but only Pennsylvania Legionnaires went to Washington to actively press the issue. Though the administration had the votes to sustain the veto, veterans and politicians from the Keystone State made their point.

In 1930, the Pennsylvania Legion concluded another successful year, in which membership exceeded 73,000. There were 567 posts, including ten chartered during the year. The Harrisburg convention closed with the election of new officers. Charles I. Engard of Philadelphia was chosen department commander, Sidney B. Martin of Pittston, western vice commander; and George J. Proesel of Dubois and Robert J. Hanna of Philadelphia, central and eastern vice commanders, respectively. Deighan and Dervin continued as adjutant and finance officer.

Throughout the interwar period, the leadership remained the Legion's anchor. Commanders served one-year appointments, and the continuing adjutant, first Deighan and later Edward A. Linsky, smoothly operated the state headquarters in Philadelphia. Prominent individuals such as George J. Proesel, Paul H. Griffith (national commander after World War II and also a member of President Truman's cabinet), and Otto F. Messner all served as Department Convention commanders. They were chosen in a manner that would spread out the benefits of thousands of conventioneers to cities and towns throughout the state. Pittsburgh and Philadelphia were chosen by the rotating Convention Committee in 1932 and 1933, while Erie, Wilkes-Barre, Johnstown, York, and Scranton hosted the convention from 1934 to 1938. Commanders came and went but adjutants served year in and year out as the chief executives of the department, touring selected posts and keeping in touch with the State Veterans' Commission in Harrisburg, the capital. With the department commander, they furthered the interests of the Legion—and the veteran—throughout the state.

In 1919, the department's Legislative Committee offered an amendment to the state constitution to provide compensation to ex-service people. This subject caused the most controversy of any issue for the Legion. Many in the nation's press called the Legion the "Treasury-looting crowd." The public and Legionnaires were divided on the matter. Lewis, then vice commander, stated at the department's fourth annual convention that he "did not think it proper nor right to come to the commonwealth of Pennsylvania as a mendicant asking alms," but he did believe in the United States taking care of the ex-serviceman and "providing adjusted compensation." His own post, Harry Ingersoll #3 of Philadelphia, was on record with about twenty others as opposing a state Bonus.

Early on, the Pennsylvania department pressed politicians for some state-financed Bonus. The *American Legion Weekly* reported that the Pennsylvania Executive Committee met on January 16, 1921, to endorse a Bonus bill providing $10 for each month of service, up to $250. The bill was submitted to the Legislature and passed unanimously. The legislative session of 1921 also proposed an amendment to the constitution. In 1923, the department's Legislative Committee again promoted an amendment to the state's constitution. The State Supreme Court ruled against the proposed amendment because the Constitution of the state of Pennsylvania had already been amended within a five-year period. A similar piece of legislation was introduced in 1927 and was unanimously passed by the House, but was never brought out of the Finance Committee of the Senate. In 1929, the department's Legislative Committee introduced an adjusted compensation bill that passed the Assembly in 1931. Finally, the issue was approved by voters in a referendum in 1933 and a series of sales taxes was passed to finance the Bonus.

The controversy over the Pennsylvania Bonus mirrored the national debate. Because some Legionnaires doubted they would survive to 1945 (the year in which all adjusted compensation certificates could be redeemed at full value by veterans of the Great War), they called the plan the "Tombstone Bonus." The agony of the Depression intensified demands for immediate payment. Finally, in September 1932, more than 18,000 Legionnaires at the annual convention in Portland, Oregon, voted to press Congress to pass an emergency Bonus act. This was the most controversial veterans' issue in these years.

The furor over the expulsion of Anthony Wayne Post #418 of Radnor typified the matter. Throughout these years, there was always a significant minority within the Legion that had disapproved of the decision to support the Bonus since 1919. Shortly after the endorsement in Portland, members of the post approved a resolution questioning "payments of gratuities to unmeriting veterans" and pledged to Hoover their "vigorous support in his present plans for economy in veterans' legislation" Post Commander Robert Gurley, an Episcopalian minister from Radnor and veteran of the Meuse-Argonne campaign, quickly emerged as the spokesman for several dissident posts, including Merion Post #445 and Post #427 in Swarthmore.

Gurley, long experienced in public affairs, seized the moment by speaking frequently to the national press. In an April 4, 1933, letter to national Commander Louis Johnson, he championed himself as the voice of the Legionnaire who was "without the opportunity or ability to make his protest heard. . . . [H]e has witnessed the high ideals of the American Legion . . . trampled in the dust of political greed. . . . In the privileges obtained . . . in the advancement of personal interest, the veteran today . . . represents a caste comparable to the worst such a system can produce." One member of the Anthony Wayne post asserted later that dissidents' actions reflected the feelings of "many members of the Legion all over the country [who] resigned as a result of the Portland convention." They were encouraged to protest the decision "by the fact that many ex-servicemen who had heretofore not been interested in the Legion or who had resigned . . . now wished to join our post, being in sympathy with our point of view."

The dissenting post quickly ran headlong into the department's leadership, which created a special committee headed by Deighan to investigate the controversy. After long deliberation, the Executive Committee suspended Post #418's charter because it had "flouted the regularly adopted policies and programs of the Legion," brought discord and dissension among Legionnaires, and defied the organization's constituted authorities. This was in direct response to a March 25, 1933, letter from Gurley and other members of the Radnor post to the *New York Herald Tribune* claiming that the Legion and the Pennsylvania department had suppressed information and tried to halt debate on the Bonus among Legionnaires.

As might be expected, the suspension of the Anthony Wayne post unleashed a storm of anti-Legion commentary from the national press. An editorial in the *Daily Times* of Radnor was headlined "Wayne Post's Expulsion Will Rock Legion Ranks" and said the dispute over the Bonus "would bring on such universal condemnation of the Legion as to jeopardize its very existence." This was typical of a segment of the nation's media at a time when veterans were made to be the scapegoats of the deepening federal budget deficit. Pennsylvania Legionnaires—and the top officials in Indianapolis—were concerned about how Gurley and others had voiced their discontent. Many felt that the Radnor post was playing into the hands of longstanding Legion opponents. Kenneth S. Franklin, commander of Post #335 in Lynbrook, New York, castigated Gurley for criticizing Legion lobbyist John Thomas Taylor, without whom "there would be little or no compensation or hospitalization for veterans." department officials also noted that more than a few members of the Radnor post had started cashing in their Bonus checks.

The matter was resolved after a long legal battle and interdepartmental conflict. The *New York Daily News* reported in June 1933 that "socially prominent members of the Anthony Wayne post . . . carried their fight against revocation of their charter to the federal courts today." The suit sought to restrain the national office from enforcing the revocation order. The fight dragged on for nearly two years. In time (and as the Bonus bill moved through Congress), the department Executive Committee asked for reinstatement of the Anthony Wayne post, pending approval by the national Executive Committee. A confidential memorandum of January 30, 1935, from Pennsylvania's Vincent A. Carroll, a national Executive Committeeman, to the national judge advocate, past national Commander James A. Drain, urged the national organization to quietly reconcile with Gurley. Carroll feared that the publicity over the lawsuit would do the American Legion great harm. "Undoubtedly," he wrote, "the group that brought this suit are fellows who have no interest in the Legion." Carroll was also concerned about the judge scheduled to hear the case: "What he would say about the defendants would not be of any moment, but what he might say about the national organization . . . might be very serious in the hands of our opponents, especially at this time." On May 14, 1935, the national Executive Committee restored #418 as a post in good standing.

The Depression had a delayed but far-reaching impact on the Legion. Like everyone, it had to cut costs. In 1930, department Commander Frank T. Pinola told Legionnaires in his annual report that the department's work was often not finished because of the comparatively low state dues—fifty cents. The department finance officer voluntarily cut his salary from $500 to $250. Other officers followed suit. The allotment for the department commander was cut from $3,000 to $2,700 (he actually had spent only $887.50 by the time of the convention in 1930). The department's officers often reminded members that Pennsylvania's budget was only $32,000, compared with more than $100,000 for the Illinois department, which had only slightly larger membership.

Despite this, the Pennsylvania Legion carried on, even flourished. A membership "roundup" initiated by the department commander raised membership to 73,049 and exceeded by more than 10,000 similar enrollment drives in Illinois and New York. Such success came in part from hard work by the Legislative Committee. In spite of hard times, the allowance for the Veterans Commission actually increased from $20,000 to $100,000 per biennium between 1930 and 1941. This was done to take care of immediate aid applications brought upon by economic conditions.

The Depression also created new concerns. Robert J. Hanna of Post #332 in the Philadelphia area complained that the Post Office Department did not even purchase replacement parts from American manufacturers. He said that the government talked of the dangers of the Depression as it kept "foreign workingmen employed when their own men who served the country are walking the streets." Other Legionnaires were outraged at individuals and institutions that seemed to benefit from the federal government. Local posts tried to get consumers and businessmen to "buy American" or to buy from local merchants. Businesses and corporate associations that opposed the Bonus were singled out for criticism, and anti-business rhetoric was common at Legion gatherings. At the 1936 state convention, Legionnaire George Earle criticized "men of great wealth [who] send us on a wild-goose chase after so-called radicals while they continue to plunder the people" and categorized as Communists "every man, woman, and child who dares to say a word which does not have the approval of Wall Street." Other Legionnaires identified with protest movements of the Thirties. The Frankford post's monthly newsletter, *Comrades,* in September 1934 noted that Communism fed on the deepening discontent of the American worker. "It is not enough for us to damn the craven activities of Communism. . . . Father [Charles] Coughlin [the 'Radio Priest' from Detroit], in opening a drive against Communism . . . maintained that there were plenty of evils under our present monetary system which made it easy for Communists to plant their seeds within the minds of good citizens." The newsletter went on to endorse Coughlin's plan for economic recovery and advocate the break-up of trusts and monopolies to ensure business opportunities for future generations.

Much of the anger felt by the rank and file was directed by the department into re-employment efforts. Beginning in 1930, post newspapers ran "economic casualty lists" of unemployed Legionnaires with short descriptions of their experience and job record. In 1932, Pennsylvania participated in the national Home Improvement Campaign, directed by Mark T. McKee, the executive director of the Legion's National Employment Commission. On April 6, Dervin submitted his first report that the department had "pledged work" worth $18,421.50. Subsequent reports pledged similar amounts, which often provided jobs "for a month or more and many of them permanent in Philadelphia County." Aiding the posts and individual Legionnaires was a post card campaign begun in the first week of July from headquarters in Philadelphia. Through the cooperation of the U.S. Employment Service, franking privileges were obtained to inform the state's homeowners of services available from unemployed veterans. More than $432,000 was pledged this way alone. On July 20, the post card campaign was extended to suburban Philadelphia.

Philadelphia's Home Improvement Campaign was modeled upon the Rochester Plan, which had been successful in upstate New York. The goal was to contact all homeowners, merchants, or tenants, seeking home improvement work for the unemployed. Legionnaires distributed pamphlets that suggested every type of improvement imaginable. Philadelphia newspapers generously covered the campaign and asked Pennsylvanians to aid the Legion, Kiwanis and Lions clubs, churches, and fraternal associations that joined. "It is not necessary that the homeowners employ veterans to do the work," a Legion publicist explained. "It is the idea of the Legion to aid every unemployed person in the county."

Legion posts were urged to reject the idea that this was a campaign of charity. Instead, it was to be considered a practical way to get needed employment to hard-pressed communities. An April 1932 editorial in *The Liaison,* a Legion publication in the Germantown section of Philadelphia, summarized the spirit and goal of the Home Improvement campaign:

> [T]he mind of an undernourished man . . . can easily be led into the fold of Communism. Poverty breeds crime. Recently, we read of two unfortunate businessmen who tried their hand at stealing, only to be caught. If God has blessed us with employment during these critical times, we should at least lend out aid to help our unfortunate neighbors. . . . If you are loyal to God and country . . . you will get behind your post to aid in destroying this national calamity that is not only threatening the sanctity of our homes but undermining our economic structure.

The significance of the employment drive was clear to participants. Throughout Pennsylvania in 1932, according to a Pittsburgh newspaper, there was "an awakening in communities formerly almost at a standstill." In Archibald, "there was no work or prospects" until the Ambrose Revel Post #328 devised a system to promote the sale of anthracite coal to other communities in Pennsylvania. The plan revived Archibald to such an extent that it was soon imitated in other coal towns in the region. The American Legion also pioneered barter arrangements (services or labor for food) between farmers and city residents in western Pennsylvania. The department's campaigns to soften the effects of unemployment did not end the Depression but did provide relief for thousands of Pennsylvanians.

The Pennsylvania Legion also worked to improve the status of World War veterans, mainly men reaching middle age in a difficult employment market. In 1938, Paul Griffith, chairman of the Employment Committee, led the fight to maintain opportunities for men over forty. "Twenty years ago," he said at a Legion convention in New York, "the flower of manhood of our nation went out in order to preserve your business and guarantee your future success. Therefore, you do owe an obligation to these men twenty years after. These men shouldn't be on relief rolls . . . but they should be employed. You say, with the most damnable of philosophy, that a man is through at forty and we of the American Legion say that the average age of him who served in the World War now is forty-three, and that man is entitled to the American standard of living. Off of the relief rolls, out of the bread lines, and employed!" This campaign extolled the virtues of the experienced man, civilian or veteran, and urged businessmen to pledge to hire a percentage of men over forty. Griffith and his commission obtained pledges from U.S. Steel, the Pennsylvania Railroad, Mellon Bank, coal companies, and others.

Pennsylvania, like other industrial states, was beset by labor disputes. Historians such as William Pencak and John Lax have revealed that the American Legion often sought to mediate labor disputes. Contrary to some perceptions, the Legion was not a strikebreaking outfit but sought to keep local posts and Legionnaires from interfering as Legion members. When Pennsylvania Legionnaires took action against unions, they usually justified it as essential to preserving law and order in their communities. In

September 1934, Legionnaires from Aliquippa placed themselves at the service of the Jones and Laughlin Steel Company when the Congress of Industrial Organizations attempted to organize the Beaver Valley area. Michael Kane, Aliquippa's chief of police, and a detachment "recruited mostly from a local Legion post clashed with CIO organizers in nearby Ambridge. One man was killed and many were injured. A union organizer recalled that some Legionnaires wore their uniforms and service caps "while doing company guard duty," open violation of Legion policy. After this incident, Kane and certain Legionnaires created the Constitutional Defense League and boasted that they had received "instruction, help, and advice" from Homer Chaillaux, director of the Legion's national Americanism Commission. Mayor Daniel Shields of Johnstown claimed that the Legion had secretly authorized drastic anti-union efforts there. Three hundred Legionnaires were deputized for special police assistance during a 1935 strike in Johnstown, but department Commander Walter Kress persuaded the Johnstown post to take no official action during the walkout. The deputized Legionnaires nonetheless retained full police powers during the strike, and other such organizations did spring up throughout the state during this time.

The theme of law and order coincided with another concern of Pennsylvania Legionnaires: that companies might shut down and move in the face of unionization. Many small and medium-sized towns across the state depended upon a main employer— a coal or steel firm, for instance. Legion posts led by small businessmen and professionals were keenly aware that communities often competed for businesses and jobs. In October 1935, a post in Scranton that had agreed to rent its hall to CIO organizers reneged after meeting with local employers. They maintained that businesses that supported the local economy would leave if their employees joined unions. Western Pennsylvania posts sponsored harmony ads in newspapers warning steelworkers that if they did not compromise with management on certain issues, the companies would move elsewhere and put thousands out of work, which eventually happened decades later. The 1937 strike at the Hershey chocolate company was illustrative. Local farmers, some of them Legionnaires, supplied the factory with more than 800,000 quarts of milk a day. They helped break a strike that had left them without a market. The town's Legion post claimed that the strike had been fomented by people "foreign to our community" who had deceived the strikers and thrown out of work "more than 4,000 men who needed to feed their families." The Associated Press reported that the post's Drum and Bugle Corps led "a brutal attack" on sit-down strikers. Corps members forced strikers to run a gauntlet as a mob beat them with sticks and clubs. The post commander insisted that, since he had no direct control of the corps, which contained many non-Legionnaires, he could not stop the action. Thereafter, department Commander Harry Colmery prohibited all Legionnaires from wearing uniforms or insignia if they served as deputies in "emergency situations."

Despite the hard times and intermittent social strife, the Legion post remained the center of community life for many veterans. An essay by William Hepworth in the February 1936 *Comrades,* the newsletter of Frankford Post #211, gives a glimpse of the average monthly meeting. Hepworth, editor of *The Frankford Dispatch,* noted the many activities designed to pull in Legionnaires. Ample entertainment was provided by Legion-sponsored glee clubs, minstrel shows, and a performance by the Post's auxiliary band, "La Petite Bugle Corps." Hepworth was impressed by the "Irish and Scotch songs, bass and tenor solos" rendered by post members during the evening. Short but effective speeches were given by the post commander on the latest bill before Congress or the Legislature in Harrisburg. A "Legion barrage," an organized flood of telegrams, had been announced earlier by the national headquarters. The issue was the Legion-endorsed Sheppard-Hill bill, which called for universal service in peacetime and the "conscription of labor and capital" in time of war. A Legionnaire and hardware store owner, Bill Kramer, conducted a "chalk talk" that humorously explained the easiest way to contact the local representative in Washington. Hepworth said he brought out "the latent energy" of the crowd and demonstrated the importance of the bill in a lively and effective manner.

However, Hepworth said his most lasting impression was the sense of purpose conveyed by all those present. "The large attendance" at the meeting should be "an inspiration to all men who are involved in other groups that are less active," he wrote. Hepworth (not a Legionnaire) enjoyed the privilege of attending meetings and felt that "all the eligibles in the Northeast should be wearing the Legion button" Clearly, the Pennsylvania Legion remained a vibrant organization nearly a decade after its inception.

The 19th annual department convention was held in York on August 19–21, 1937. William F. Smith was selected as the 1937–38 department commander. Smith, described as "Punxsutawney's gift to the Legion," was born on April 7, 1888, at Gurnel in Tioga County. He grew up there and attended the State Teachers' College in Indiana, Pennsylvania, serving as the school's baseball, football, and basketball coach from 1913–17. During World War I, Smith sought to enter the Second Officers' Training School at Fort Oglethorpe, Georgia. The quota for officers had been filled when he arrived, so he returned to Pennsylvania and in February 1918 enlisted in the Army as a private. He was commissioned as a sergeant within nineteen days and eventually became a second lieutenant of infantry. He was honorably discharged in December and continued in the Reserve for nearly a decade as a first lieutenant of infantry.

After his discharge in 1922, Smith joined Post #62 and became a member of the Blair County Voiture #350 of the Forty and Eight. He served on several membership and employment committees and was named post commander in 1932. Smith became commander of the 27th District in 1934 and western vice commander in 1935. In 1936, he served as chairman of the department's Employment Committee, and in 1937 was unanimously elected department commander.

The York convention was a prelude to what was later described as the greatest of the national conventions, the New York gathering in 1937. It opened on September 20 with more than 15,000 Pennsylvania Legionnaires in attendance. Each of the state's thirty-six districts sent delegates. They helped elect Daniel J. Doherty of Massachusetts as national commander. The convention closed with an eighteen-hour parade with 150,000 Legionnaires passing in review, including 10,000 Pennsylvanians. The Keystone State also contributed thirty-five bands and ninety drum and bugle corps, and the "grand voiture" of Pennsylvania sent about 1,200 Voyageurs to march in the largest Forty and Eight parade ever. The Keystone State's delegation won trophies for the most musical organizations in line and the largest delegation in line.

Smith's tenure was marked by innovation as well as close attention to tradition. He continued to promote adjutants' and commanders' meetings across major regions of the state and emphasized the celebration of Armistice Day, with local parades, parties, and banquets. The annual membership drive was kicked off at the "roundup" in Harrisburg in December, where caravans from all over the department converged. As was the custom, awards were given to posts that had signed up the most members and booby prizes were created for those that showed the least initiative or success. More than 38,000 new members were signed up, with 150 of the 628 posts going "over the top" of the goal set by the department adjutant and his staff for new members. The department consistently was over the top in national membership drives throughout the 1930s.

The following months showed the depth and breadth of Legion activity in a year. At the beginning of the year, Pennsylvania's national committeeman participated in discussions ranging from rehabilitation to national defense to universal service. February saw the department's Americanism Committee conduct some of its most important business, including the administration of flag code education, Americanism Award medals, and essay contests. Throughout the department, local Americanism chairmen supervised the celebration of February 12 (Lincoln's birthday) and February 22 (Washington's birthday). These featured lectures and radio talks on defense and patriotism themes. In March, the Keystone State's 12th District played host to the national Americanism chairman, Homer Chaillaux. His address on Americanism from the Irem Temple in Wilkes-Barre was broadcast nationwide over a hookup arranged by Tom Williams, the department's national defense chairman.

March 15 was the Legion's nineteenth birthday. Most posts held dinners while listening to national Commander Doherty over NBC. The following night, the department put together a full entertainment and informational program. Under the auspices of the Irwin post, the message and pageantry of the Pennsylvania Legion was broadcast statewide over KDKA in Pittsburgh. Entertainment was provided by the Duquesne Drum and Bugle Corps and speeches on patriotism and national sacrifice were given by department commander Smith and Sally Homer, president of the auxiliary. Listeners also heard how the Legion supported youth activities (especially Legion baseball) and how it sustained worthy causes in the local community and state.

In the meantime, the less conspicuous but just as important activities of the Pennsylvania department continued. During an Executive Committee meeting on April 2, 1938, committee reports were submitted to Smith. According to meeting minutes, "The committee took a firm stand against Communism, Naziism and Fascism, and Commander Smith delivered another of his now-famous attacks on subversive groups." Also publicized was the department's work on the Service Caravan, which traveled throughout the state investigating service claims, child labor, and the status of veterans in public works programs. The caravan also answered questions on hospitalization, medical treatment, the Bonus, and insurance. J. Guy Griffith, organizer of the caravan, warned that some hospitals then occupied by World War veterans might soon be used for wounded military personnel. In a few years, the warning seemed eerily prophetic.

On April 7, the department was toured by Doherty, who visited Scranton, Pottsville, Harrisburg, and Philadelphia. In these and other towns he spoke on Americanism and national defense. On April 8, the department exceeded 60,000 members, topping the goal set earlier in the year. The Sons of the American Legion celebrated its fifth anniversary in May as more posts reported new squadrons every month. Legionnaires also pitched in during community emergencies; Bradford Post #108 helped look for a girl lost in the woods of western Pennsylvania, supplied food to the search party, and offered a $200 reward to anyone successful in the search.

For a week before Memorial Day, the Legion's official flower, the poppy, was seen all over Pennsylvania. Virtually every post and the Legion Auxiliary distributed 1 million poppies "in every nook and cranny of the state, again reminding the public that there was such a thing as the World War and that something more than money was lost on the battlefields of Europe by America," according to records of the 1938 convention. Poppy sales replenished the welfare funds of the Legion posts and guaranteed continued help for many veterans and their families. With veterans of the Civil War and the Spanish-American War, Legionnaires decorated the graves of the fallen with flags and flowers. July 2, 1938, saw some of the few survivors of the Civil War gather for the seventy-fifth anniversary of the battle of Gettysburg. General Pershing and Doherty attended.

The daily activities of the many posts in Pennsylvania showed the extent to which they had become part of the state and local community. As hostile a critic as writer John Dos Passos, who had condemned the American Legion in his *USA Trilogy*, noted that the Legion was a vital part of the "folk life of America." The Keystone Legion during the Great Depression was a testament to that.

CHAPTER

4

WAR AND CONFLICT

The Next Generation of Pennsylvania Veterans, 1940–54

The period 1940–54 saw great change in the Pennsylvania American Legion. World War II provided a new generation of servicemen eligible for membership. More than that, the advent of the "American century" and Cold War fears created new Legion activities and enhanced the value of existing ones. The Keystone Legion was tested in war and peace. Colorful and effective figures such as John Thomas Taylor, Paul Griffith, and Walter Allesandroni helped to guide Legion policy and protect veterans' rights and interests in Pennsylvania.

The Legion urged Americans to stay aloof of problems in Europe. Contrary to accusations of war-mongering, the Legion was one of the last major opinion makers to support American entrance into another European war.

In their speeches and writings, Pennsylvania Legionnaires clearly gave their feelings. "Having carried the major part of the burden . . . the ex-servicemen . . . know better than anyone else the futility of any attempt by Americans to settle European disputes," read one resolution passed at the department convention in 1940. The resolution also stated that Legionnaires recognized that "propaganda emanating from the warring nations will have a tendency to develop un-neutrality on our part. . . . Our post proposes that the Legion use its strength and influence to promote and encourage an aggressive counter-education program." Several posts, particularly in the Pittsburgh area, claimed to have exceeded their 1940 membership quotas because of their participation in the anti-war campaign. Still, while Legionnaires were not united in their stand on the war, they certainly feared aggression in Asia and Europe.

The debate over America's entrance into World War II was mooted by the Japanese attack on Pearl Harbor on December 7, 1941. The Legion sprang into action. Posts served as community liaisons with the FBI, the War Department, and the Selective Service System. Shortly, the Keystone Legion became an indispensable part of the war effort.

Familiar with the idea of "total war," the Legion pledged full cooperation with the War Department to mobilize the entire population. Starting in 1940, more than two-thirds of draft board members throughout Pennsylvania were Legionnaires. The department participated in the state's Aircraft Warning Service observation posts. Under Adjutant Edward Linsky, 1,200 posts operated twenty-four hours a day in a service that required 40,000 observers. The Legion helped the FBI and military intelligence round up people suspected of enemy activity. Even before the war, Legion posts reported on Bund meetings in their areas and later helped to locate and intern Bund members. The Bund was a German-American, pre-Nazi organization active in the Midwest and Northeast of the United States. It was labeled as un-American and dangerous by both the FBI and the House Un-American Activities Committee. The Legion recognized that, though the conflict was fought far beyond America's shores, its demands were always great. In 1943, the Keystone Legion collected more than 20,000 junked cars for scrap. It led the nation in collecting old vinyl records to be turned into rubber. In cooperation with the auxiliary, it raised $8 million for new submarines. In 1944, at the suggestion of the commander of the Variety Post in Philadelphia, a plan was developed to co-operate with the movie industry to sell war bonds. Boys and girls throughout the state were asked to register with a theater in their area and participate in the drive. By the end of the year, more than 18,000 children had done so. Nearly $7 million in bonds were sold in the fourth war loan drive. In conjunction with Pennsylvania's Department of Education, the Keystone Legion organized the Victory Corps program, which asked high school boys and teachers to participate in weekend military drills and instruction.

Though the nation was united in the effort, problems emerged as the war dragged on. The Pennsylvania Legion helped to mediate labor disputes in a pledge to keep industrial production going at full throttle. A railroad strike was narrowly averted in 1944 when the Pennsylvania department joined others in the state in urging a quick settlement. Legion posts also stood up for the rights of labor when they felt that they had been assaulted. South Fork Post #653 passed a motion authorizing its commander, during the upcoming department convention, to protest national Commander Roscoe Waring's criticism of "John L. Lewis and all for which he stands," a reference to CIO complaints about wages and working conditions during the war. Department officials eventually persuaded Waring to tone down his remark and not resort to union bashing.

Clearly, the war strengthened and reinvigorated the Pennsylvania Legion. In 1945, the national historian and curator sent out a questionnaire to every department. The response of the Pennsylvania Legion, examined piece by piece, gives a cross-section of the veterans' organization at the time and demonstrates its strength during the Second World War.

Re-incorporated in December 1940 to obtain financing on its new mortgage for its headquarters, the Keystone Legion was the third-largest department in the country, with more than 100,000 members. The average delegation sent to annual national conventions during the war was about 4,000. Also during war years, state conventions were attended by 20,000 to 25,000 Legionnaires. The department prided itself on having more than 200 drum and bugle corps at most of the pre-war conventions. Pennsylvania's Sons of the Legion led the nation in membership with 6,500, an increase of more than 1,000 from 1943. The report cited the Legion affiliate's work in bond drives and Americanism. Many of the young men would become members of the next generation of the Legion.

The report suggested that the Legion's overall image in the state was high. It remarked that the state Legion had satisfactory relations with organized labor and excellent relations with other civic groups such as the Rotary and Kiwanis clubs. Indeed, the Legion in Pennsylvania had worked hard to improve relations with the labor movement through the joint promotion of war bond drives and victory rallies. Linsky noted that the Depression had "very little influence except that [the] unemployment was tremendous." Perhaps, in 1945, "hard times" had become a distant memory.

By 1940, there were about fifteen African-American posts registered by the Department of Pennsylvania. The Keystone Legion was tied with Oklahoma and second only to North Carolina in the number of these posts at the time. The three largest were the Henry C. Williams Post of McKeesport with 666 members, the William Dempsy Post of Aliquippa with 647 members, and the Joseph H. Ford Post of Monessen with 618 members. The smallest were the Crispus Attucks Post of Pittsburgh with thirty members and the Lincoln Post of Philadelphia with nine. Regardless of size, each post sponsored activities and programs for veterans and youth in their communities.

A story from West Chester illustrates the image of the American Legion among African-Americans at the time. To celebrate the installation of a new post commander on October 16, 1940, the Nathan Holmes Post #362 of West Chester organized a parade in which Legionnaires, members of the local chapter of the National Association for the Advancement of Colored People, and African-American business people participated. The day's highlight was a speech by the visiting national commander, Raymond J. Kelly of Michigan, who summarized his year in office and stressed his role "in the fight for recognition of Negroes in the Army, Navy, and National Guard." He also said that the Holmes post and other Negro posts had been important in the fight for Bonus legislation and predicted they would play a significant role in the days ahead.

The new Holmes post commander was Horace V. Pippin. He was born in Goshen, New York, and worked as a laborer until 1917, when he enlisted in the infantry in World War I. Upon his discharge, he and his wife settled in West Chester, where he joined the Holmes post. A long-time friend recalled that he was "a friendly man who worked with the Boy Scouts for many years, and he kept the children in his neighborhood interested in going to school." He also spoke fondly of his military service and worked as post commander in war preparedness and mobilization campaigns. Pippin also was an accomplished artist. In the 1930s, he was recognized by many critics as a self-taught primitivist whose paintings, including "The Barracks," "The Park Bench," and a collection consisting of three paintings of John Brown and four of the Holy Mountain, expressed hope and unity in exceptional style. In 1937, after a showing of several of his works, he "was acclaimed as the greatest black painter of his time," according to his newspaper obituary in 1988.

After Pearl Harbor, the war consumed most of the energy of local posts. Aside from other concerns, the Legion made every effort to contact the new generation of servicemen. Posts also offered entertainment for servicemen on furlough. "Every post has open house at meetings [for new veterans or off-duty servicemen]. . . . Several canteens [have] been established throughout the state." During the war, the department was visited by governors from every state as well as President Roosevelt.

The strength of the Pennsylvania Legion at the time was easily seen in the sheer variety of posts across the state. Ten posts, all in the Pittsburgh and Philadelphia areas, reported memberships of 1,000 or more; eight in the same areas of the state had memberships of 800 or more. The bulk of the membership, its real strength, lay in the small and medium-sized posts: 166 had 120 to 250 members; sixty-five had fifty-one to 125 members; 171 reported fewer than fifty. A delegation from national headquarters in Indianapolis was surprised that many posts already had "burned the mortgage" on their buildings.

Posts differed in composition as well. There was a fluctuating number (seventeen were recorded in 1945) of "labor" posts (composed entirely of union members), posts composed of civil servants, "railroad" posts, and others devoted to a specific industry or business. There also were five posts made up exclusively of women, mainly former military nurses. All posts held meetings twice a month, conducted youth programs, and attempted to get involved in their community.

From 1940–44, conventions were held in Reading, Altoona, Pittsburgh, Wilkes-Barre, and Harrisburg, respectively. In 1945, finally because of wartime restrictions, no formal convention was held. During the war, the department also moved its headquarters from Philadelphia to Harrisburg. The 1944 gathering was typical of the wartime conventions. Harrisburg was engulfed by an entirely new—and temporary—population. Hotels and inns used in the past for Legion conventions were, according to 1944 convention proceedings, "cramped by Army camps and the necessary personnel that goes with [them], by numerous manufacturing of wartime industries, so that we now have 120,000 in population." Legion families, especially those in the surrounding communities, had already agreed to share their homes with Army depot workers and itinerant servicemen in need of temporary shelter. For the first time in years, many Legionnaires themselves bivouacked in nearby parks and fields.

Adjutant Linsky's report centered on aid to the state's men and women in service. In 1943, the department approved $100,000 to purchase cigarettes through the state office. They were bought through major tobacco companies, which offered a donation of a 10 percent discount, then were sent to servicepeople across the globe. The packages contained the message, "Compliments of the American Legion and the American Legion Auxiliary, Department of Pennsylvania."

The campaign was so well received that the Legion office got thank-you letters from veterans overseas. One came from George N. Carpenter, a former state representative who was an Army corporal stationed "somewhere in the Pacific." The letter simply read:

> Received this card out of a carton of cigarettes and was glad to receive them. . . . I have been a [Legion] member for a number of years. Am a charter member of Post #514

in Bushkill, Pa.; also was the second commander of said
post and served in the AEF in World War I.

Now I am out on an island. . . . It is not so good out
here for the men of my age because it is hard for us to
take it, but we manage to get along some way.

Thank God for the Legion and the people of Pennsylvania. You have been a great help to the morale of us all.

Mrs. Harry W. Piper was the president of the Legion Auxiliary
of Pennsylvania in 1943–44. Her tenure epitomized the success
of the women's organization. For three straight years, the Auxiliary brought its membership to the goal of 53,800. Its activities
were significant and diverse, including child welfare work, legislative lobbying for the GI Bill, countless bond drives, and the
donation of $1,600 for the Junior Baseball program.

The Forty and Eight, the department's "fun and honor" group,
reached its highest membership ever, at 5,000. It concentrated
on solving the problems of juvenile delinquency. John W. Kinsey,
chairman of the Sons of the Legion, warned not to neglect the
problems of youth. "We of the Legion should give these boys a little more of our time. . . . There are too many Posts lagging and
passing up the Sons. They are making a mistake, for men of the
Legion don't forget that Hitler got his start by organizing the
youth of Germany." Legionnaires were also properly chided for
not taking seriously enough social welfare work and supporting
the education of orphans at the Scotland School.

Governor Edward Martin, a fellow Legionnaire, gave a speech
at the 1944 convention affirming the GI Bill and the principle of
veterans' benefits. "We want a country," he stated, "where a
man can provide for his family, build a home, educate his children and provide for his own security. This is the American way.
We do not want a Communistic country where men are limited,
regimented, marched and counter-marched. We want a free
country, where the government governs all men alike." Martin
concluded by both supporting the war effort and saying that
"government must keep out of business."

One of the resolutions passed—at the urging of women whose
sons had been killed in service, the "Gold Star Mothers"—
demanded the "immediate revocation of all regulations by the
State and War departments granting these special privileges and

coddling of these war prisoners." The Pennsylvania department would urge the National Executive Committee and the Legion's lobbyists in Washington to introduce appropriate legislation on the matter.

Abram Orlow, a Legionnaire and chairman of the southeastern district of Pennsylvania's B'nai B'rith, recognized the work of the Pennsylvania Legion "because of its outstanding courage and because of its outstanding understanding of the rights of minorities." Both groups pledged to wage an anti-discrimination campaign around the theme "To Bigotry, No Sanction." Likeminded Legion resolutions included an item, introduced by the Lincoln Post #89, that condemned the record of certain departments (especially in the South) for barring membership to veterans on racial grounds as "unjust and un-democratic." The resolution was unanimously passed at the convention. In the coming years, the Pennsylvania department led in the fight against the exclusionary policies of certain southern departments.

The keynote address was given by past national Commander Louis Johnson, currently at work in the War Department. He reminded Legionnaires of the organization's early advocacy of preparedness. "If this country had followed the mandates of the American Legion and put into action its National Defense Program, I don't believe there would be any world war today or that Hitler would ever have dared march," he said. Johnson added that the United States would have to continue to play a pivotal role in world affairs. "It was the big nations . . . that balled up things in the last peace era. . . . In the early days it will be the big nations that will have to take the lead here and then bring in the little nations with them." Johnson cited the emergence of new aircraft and military technology that made America's previous security a thing of the past. This would ensure "not one Pearl Harbor but fifty or more Pearl Harbors" if international events were ignored by future presidents. Johnson concluded that the American Legion would support "an association of nations without surrendering the sovereignty of their nation one whit."

The aftermath of the war was also on the minds of Legionnaires. James P. Murray, chairman of the department Americanism Commission, warned them of the potential problems of demobilization. "Let us all recognize," he maintained, "that we as Americans are willing to give up a lot of things. . . . Let it be understood that these are duration measures and restrictions, and we want them removed ASAP when we win this war." For Legionnaires, the best government was one that was as lean and efficient as possible.

Future programs and entitlements for veterans were concerns. Charles A. Aurer, chairman of the department's Legislative Committee and the postwar Planning Commission, urged posts to strongly lobby for the GI Bill. "It is up to the Legion to take the leadership after the war as we took after the First World War. . . . We took the leadership in formulating and having passed the GI Bill. . . . The federal government had to pass the GI Bill and it was a Legion bill and if we sell that kind of service as we have to sell under this GI Bill, your membership will follow as the night follows the day."

The *American Legion Monthly* of March 1945 reported that plans for re-absorbing Pennsylvania's GIs were well under way. In Pittsburgh, the task of giving jobs to nearly 400,000 servicemen was coordinated by public and private efforts. A coalition of Legion service officers, representative of the United States Employment Service and large private industries, forged several interlocking programs. Industries such as U.S. Steel catalogued and publicized the jobs disabled veterans could perform. Legion service officers provided employment counsel and information on vocational training. As in peacetime, Legionnaires also represented veterans who were having difficulties with the Veterans Administration in receiving cash benefits. Of the 7,500 veterans who returned to the Pittsburgh area before the war ended, nearly 1,000 received some vocational training.

Still, the admission of another group of veterans into an organization exclusively designed for AEF veterans was troublesome. The Pennsylvania department, like the national organization, was ambivalent about opening its ranks. Some, like future national Commander Paul Griffith, maintained that Legion principles demanded that World War II veterans be admitted "to ensure the stability of America." Others countered that the interests of men who averaged forty-nine years of age would clash with their counterparts of 1941–45 who averaged about 28 years of age. Ultimately, the interests of both groups were shown to be similar.

Despite generational differences, veterans of both wars could identify with a common foe. Syndicated columnist Damon Runyon wrote in early 1942 that many former doughboys considered World War II to be simply "a continuation of their old World War." Pennsylvania veterans expressed similar feelings. An editorial written by a Legionnaire in an Erie newspaper noted that Hitler had been a corporal in the German imperial army "and was now a nightmare far worse than any of us could have envisioned in 1918." Future department Commander Walter Allesandroni was reminded of his Legionnaire uncle who had warned him of the dangers of an expansionistic Germany and the "iron grip of Mussolini" in his former homeland, Italy. The Japanese attack on Pearl Harbor confirmed in the minds of many veterans that isolation "was a greater danger to the future of America's veterans than three kaisers combined," according to Eric Fisher Wood. The consensus among World War I veterans was that the men who had "finished the job" should be allowed to join the nation's largest veterans' organization.

The Keystone Legion was adamant in its support of the rights of all veterans. "We do not want and we must not have a dole, a WPA job or an insufficient subsistence charity," read a joint statement from the Pennsylvania Legion and its Auxiliary. "The members of our armed forces have given up . . . all the things we are enjoying here at home. They have a right to expect a job, a position, a retraining . . . a right to make an honest living sufficient to adequately maintain themselves and families when they return." Veterans were concerned with "devising ways and means of helping veterans of both world wars and to be gainfully employed rather than having to seek jobs on a glorified WPA." The Pennsylvania Legion's legislative agenda for 1945 aimed at changing workers' compensation laws to remove any hindrance to veterans with medical discharges, revising civil service laws to permit orphaned children and the wives of totally disabled veterans to take jobs, and affirming veterans' preference on all future public works programs.

Individual posts often led the way in bringing in new members. The James Farrel Post #330 of Waynesburg, a rural post of 337 members in a town of 5,000, started a campaign that later became a model for the department. A department pamphlet, "At

Home," described the process of recruitment in detail. Even during induction, young servicemen were provided with essentials that "didn't cost the soldier a dime." They were given Gideon Bibles, "a couple of packages of cigarettes and a box lunch to eat" as they got on the bus. These young men were sold on the proposition that "the American Legion is [in] back of them."

When possible, Legion posts organized parties for the departing sons of Waynesburg. Soldiers, sailors, and Marines often received free "pony editions" (without advertising) of the *American Legion Magazine* from their home state. When they returned on furlough or after an honorable discharge, they were treated to free food, free beer, and free entertainment. As the war proceeded, returned veterans were brought in as speakers. Legion representatives presented certificates to families who had lost relatives. By 1945, Legion initiation ceremonies of twenty to forty-five veterans at a time were being regularly conducted. These men proved to be able recruiters, bringing young veterans into the James Farrel Post through example and action.

"Veterans of World War II are becoming Legion conscious, as many claims coming through have power of attorney in favor of our organization," said a Legion service officer from Allentown after meeting with a group of recently discharged servicemen in his area. An article in the March 1947 issue of the *American Legion Magazine,* "Why I Joined the Legion," contained a number of interviews with new Pennsylvania members. Many emphasized family ties and membership in Legion youth groups. Roger W. Fuhrman of York joined a local post because "I knew the Legion was a good organization that helped the veterans of the First World War, because my grandfather was a veteran of that war and joined the Legion, and because Legionnaires had helped me to play baseball as a kid." Another recounted how he had changed his views about joining when he received unsolicited Christmas cards and gifts from Legion-sponsored efforts. Veterans of the Second World War were interested in the rights of veterans and how the Legion would secure the goals they had fought for. Some expressed a fear of Communism, other wished to work with youth or the disabled, and still others hoped that the Legion would preserve the spirit of sacrifice and comradeship that had developed during the war. James P. Lutz of Bristol summarized the feelings of many when he said the Legion "should be strong enough to do anything we wanted for our own and for the welfare of our country." The next generation of Legion leadership would try to put into practice such feelings and attitudes.

For many, the biggest reason to join the Legion was its unyielding support for the GI Bill. The groundwork laid by the "Legion lobby" before World War II accelerated efforts to aid the new GIs. Everyone from President Roosevelt on down had ideas about aiding discharged servicemen, but it was the Legion that put together what Senator Ralph Yarborough later termed "the most foresighted veterans' program in history." A comprehensive package, the GI Bill provided home and farm mortgage loans, free medical care, unemployment insurance, disability allowances, and vocational and college educations to nearly 15 million men. The fact that so many men had sacrificed years of their lives created an overwhelming obligation on the part of the federal government.

Most responsible for laying the groundwork for the GI Bill was John Thomas Taylor, a lawyer, soldier, long-time Legionnaire, and native Pennsylvanian. Chairman of the Legion's national Executive Committee for thirty years, Taylor appeared in a 1935 cover story of *Time* magazine as the lobbyist who had "put three presidents in their place." He made decisions, great and small, affecting millions of veterans and their dependents. "The veterans' lobby?" he once quipped to a reporter's question. "You're looking at it. I'm it."

Politics and service were Taylor's lifeblood. He was the son of a police chief and leading Republican in Philadelphia. He attended Temple University, took a law degree at the University of Pennsylvania, and did two years of post-graduate work at the Inns of Court in London. He got his early training in the ins and outs of Congress, when in 1914 he became secretary to Pennsylvania Senator Boise Penrose, the state's reputed political boss. On the day that the United States entered World War I, Taylor left a six-year law practice to enlist in the Army. He served as captain in the 79th Infantry Division for seventeen months in the defense of Verdun as well as in the Argonne and Aisne-Marne offensives. Taylor earned thirteen decorations during this time. In 1919, he attended the Paris Caucus, then returned to his camp in Germany to spread the word about the Legion. Ten days after returning to the United States, he witnessed the signing of the Legion's articles of incorporation by President Wilson. Taylor took up the Legion's legislative battles in Washington with his former law partner, Thomas W. Miller. At that time, his offices were temporary headquarters for the Legion; there was first published the *American Legion Weekly*, and there the Legion's first legislative activities began. In 1920, Taylor solely assumed the role of chief Legion lobbyist, a position he held until his retirement in 1950.

Taylor was always a point of controversy. Through his efforts, the Legion became a major player in national affairs. Taylor, according to Washington columnist Drew Pearson, was "never befuddled by lengthy resolutions" passed at Legion conventions and often devised "a legislative program which he thinks the Legion ought to have, then he proceeds to push it through." Still, Taylor got enacted, often over veto, bills dealing with the Bonus, veterans' benefits, and national defense. As early as 1924, the Legion's manual was able to boast: "The Legion has extracted from Congress in one year more than the Yanks of '61 and '65 were able to get in more than thirty years and more than the Spanish-American veterans in the first ten years."

Taylor's efforts proved to be vital to the Legion; from 1919–33, the federal government spent more than $5½ billion on veterans' affairs. On the average, $1 out of every $4 that Uncle Sam spent slipped into a veteran's pocket. The first significant legislation Taylor worked on was the Sweet bill, which increased the total disability compensation of World War I veterans to $100 a month. There followed legislation that spent an initial $18 million for hospitals and the ninety-four other facilities of the Veterans Administration.

As a Reserve officer, Taylor, like many first-generation Legionnaires, re-entered service when the nation was again threatened by war. In September 1941, en route to the national convention, he was named assistant to the director of the War Department's Bureau of Public Relations. In that position, Taylor had to organize Army emergency relief to drafters "who found themselves in dire financial straits," according to the *American Legion Magazine*. To this end, he helped organize the U.S.

Army-sponsored Irving Berlin show "This Is the Army," raising nearly $17 million.

Taylor's second career in the military was as colorful as his Legion service. One day, he ran into an old friend who was preparing for the November 1942 invasion of North Africa. He asked Taylor to go with him, and Taylor seized the opportunity. He landed with the advance echelon of the Western Task Force that took Casablanca, Morocco. Almost immediately, according to *Stars and Stripes,* Taylor was sent on a 1,800-mile journey through the desert to persuade Arab chieftains and French Foreign Legion posts to cooperate with the Allies.

Thereafter, Taylor was assigned to Allied publicity work. He traveled to Algiers, Algeria, and Tunis, Tunisia, with Lieutenant General George S. Patton Jr., acting as liaison between American and British forces. These assignments were soon followed by the Sicilian campaign and the landing at Salerno, Italy. After viewing an eruption of Mount Vesuvius (an event Taylor's friends attributed to his arrival on the scene), Taylor moved northward, past Naples and Anzio, to just beyond Rome. When a new task force was created to land in southern France with the Seventh Army, Taylor was with it. He accompanied the invasion force from San Raphael to Toulon to the triumphant capture of Marseilles. Taylor was with the French First Army when Strasbourg was taken and was made a private first class in the French Foreign Legion. During these campaigns, Taylor reacquainted himself with the average soldier and received, in his own words, "an intimate knowledge of just what the new boys of World War II are thinking about." Taylor learned that, much like their fathers, the GIs worried most about a safe return to work and family. This helped Taylor formulate new legislation for veterans.

As before, the Keystone Legion worked hardest for veterans with the most obvious needs. In 1946, according to department convention proceedings, a coalition of Legion service officers, the State Veterans' Commission, and public officials called "attention to the fact that [while] we have 1 million in the armed forces of the United States from Pennsylvania," the Keystone State had only two major veterans' hospitals, with sick and injured veterans still housed at the Naval Hospital in Philadelphia and in surrounding states. The group simply urged that the number of hospitals and beds be on par with the state's population. This would be a continual fight in the decades after World War II.

One of Pennsylvania's Legionnaires who fought for change, and the first national commander (1946–47) from the state since Franklin D'Olier, was Paul H. Griffith. During his term, the American Legion dealt with housing and health care for veterans of both world wars. His connections with the Truman administration and national politics proved indispensable to Legion legislative efforts.

Griffith was born on April 8, 1897, in Uniontown. When the United States entered World War I, he left high school to enlist in the Army. He became a non-commissioned officer in Company D, 110th Infantry and 55th Infantry Brigade Headquarters of the famous 28th Division. Griffith fought in the Champagne-Marne and the Meuse-Argonne campaigns as well as in a number of defensive sectors. He earned the Silver Star, the Purple Heart, the Legion of Honor, and the Croix de Guerre.

Griffith was active in the Legion from its inception and eventually served in practically every capacity in his post, the department, and the national organization. He was a long-time member of Lafayette Post #51 in Uniontown and served as the post commander in 1928. Despite his far-ranging activities, he found the time, according to his campaign biography, "to become one of the best buglers in the nationally famous Uniontown Drum and Bugle Corps." Griffith worked with his father as a dairy wholesaler in Pennsylvania and West Virginia. In the early 1920s, he was accused of watering his milk. In 1946, a Harrisburg journalist described the results of the case:

> He [Griffith] was advised by his legal counsel to emphatically deny, over and over, that he had added any water. After his acquittal, he was heard to whisper to his lawyer, "Gosh, it's lucky for me the judge didn't ask if I had added any *milk* to the *water!*" From then on, he was known throughout the state as "Doc."

Rising through the Legion ranks, he was elected department commander in 1932–33. Griffith's chief interest through all these years was the Legion's rehabilitation program for injured and disabled veterans. He helped write the Four-Point Program, which restored benefits to thousands of disabled veterans after the Economy Act of 1933, specifically: (1) restoration of previous payment rates for disabled veterans; (2) the return of more than thirty thousand "presumptive" cases (tuberculosis and mental illness) to relief rolls; (3) the restoration of free hospitalization for all veterans; and (4) more aid for widows and orphans of all servicemen. Griffith was chairman of the national Americanism Commission in 1934 and director of the national employment and veterans' preference committees from 1937–44. He was director of the Washington office (the lobbying branch of national headquarters) for a number of years after the war. In June 1940, Griffith was one of the first Reserve officers to request assignment to active duty—realizing that American involvement in World War II was inevitable. As a major, he served two years overseas and two more as an assistant executive in the office of the undersecretary of war. Griffith worked closely with fellow Legionnaire Louis Johnson (a former South Dakota senator and secretary of war) to coordinate industrial mobilization and negotiate all War Department contracts.

"True to the cardinal principles of the Legion," Griffith worked on matters concerning the young veterans returning home. "His two-fisted fight for legislation guaranteeing veterans reinstatement in their old jobs," stated a Legion press release, "won for him the Army's Legion of Merit." On February 2, 1942, he was promoted to the rank of lieutenant colonel. The next month, he was appointed the military member of an American fact-finding mission to India. According to his campaign biography, he also participated on "various missions and secret assignments from the jungles of Burma to the deserts of North Africa" and in every theater of operation. Upon his return to the United States, Griffith was transferred to the Selective Service System, where he worked with General Lewis Hershey.

After the war and more than five years of active duty, Griffith was released from active service. He re-entered service as a major, soon rose to the rank of colonel, and retired as a brigadier general. Griffith continued his work on behalf of veterans when in 1945 he was nominated as a Legion representative to the national commission to study the GI Bill of Rights.

The Forties and Fifties saw the retirement or death of significant members of the Pennsylvania Legion. David J. Davis, department commander in 1931 and a prominent Scranton attorney, died in 1943. So did William F. Smith of Punxsutawney, the department commander in 1937 and a long-time member of the John Jacob Fisher Post. On June 1, 1953, Edward A. Linsky, department adjutant for more than eighteen years, retired due to ill health. He was succeeded by Daniel W. Shaub of Harrisburg, who had come to department headquarters in 1944 as rehabilitation director. The department had its share of tragedies as well. On August 28, 1949, the department Commander Edward J. Cosgrove apparently committed suicide. He formerly had been head of the Koch-Conley Post, Scranton's largest.

By the summer of 1950, the growth of the Keystone Legion was evident everywhere. Veterans of Leyte Gulf, Iwo Jima, and the Normandy beaches rubbed shoulders with survivors of the Chateau-Thierry and Argonne offensives. According to the department's 1950 convention corporation president, the Pennsylvania Legion's annual meeting was larger than the national convention of either major political party. In addition to more than 9,000 delegates from the department and its Auxiliary, 60,000 spouses and other visitors came to Philadelphia for the convention. For eleven years after World War II, the department convention alternated between Philadelphia and Pittsburgh, since these were the only cities big enough to accommodate such gatherings.

The Pennsylvania department, the Legion's largest, passed resolutions on the Korean conflict, national defense, "militant opposition to Communism wherever it appears," and a dozen other issues facing veterans and the nation. Senators Francis J. Myers and Edward Martin as well as Governor James H. Duff spoke during the three-day convention. There was spirited competition among fifty drum and bugle corps at Municipal Stadium on August 11. The convention wound up the next day with a five-hour parade.

The main focus, however, was on the last appearance as department commander of Allesandroni. He was the first World War II veteran elected Pennsylvania commander. At thirty-six, he was the youngest man to serve in the position. A graduate of

Villanova College and the University of Pennsylvania Law School, he began to rise when he became associated with Judge Robert E. Lamberton. When Lamberton was elected mayor of Philadelphia, Allesandroni served as his secretary at City Hall. During World War II, he volunteered for Marine service. He attained the rank of captain and later became an assistant chief of staff with a commanding general in the Pacific.

Upon his return, Allesandroni joined the Russell C. Gross Post #562 in Philadelphia. He was a delegate to the Philadelphia County Committee on Veterans' Hospitals and was a member of the Legion's national Naval Affairs Committee. In 1948, Allesandroni was named chairman of the Legion's national Housing Committee. On the recommendation of Pennsylvania's last national vice commander, Edward R. Stirling (1940–41), he was elected to that position at the Miami convention that year. Long a fighter for low-cost veterans' housing, Allesandroni led a minority caucus at various Legion gatherings in support of the Taft-Ellender-Wagner bill. He lobbied hard for inexpensive housing for students at Pennsylvania State University and other institutions where the GI Bill was taking effect. After a two-year struggle, his minority report became the Legion's position on low-cost housing, and he testified before Congress in support of the bill. This victory allowed veterans across the country to reap benefits first provided in Pennsylvania.

All was not smooth sailing for Allesandroni. While his youth and vigor made him a natural leader for many new Legionnaires, he posed a challenge to more than a few members of the department's "old guard." As a result, Allesandroni had a tough struggle when he sought the position of state commander in 1949, though he won overwhelmingly. Pennsylvania, unlike many other departments, increased its membership (by more than 8 percent) during the next twelve months.

Allesandroni made national headlines by heading the Legion's Tide for Toys campaign. It was designed to add some humanity to the fight against Communism in Europe. By the end of the year, 3 million toys had been collected for the deprived children of Western Europe. Pennsylvania easily exceeded its nearest competitor, New York, in toys collected and donated more than thirty other departments combined. An account of the campaign in Shippensburg stated that the toys "constituted a more effective tactic against Stalin . . . than any form of political grandstanding or military maneuver." On September 8, 1951, Commander Aloysius O'Donnell of the Alfred Stevenson Post #190 was honored by the Chester chapter of the American Newspaper Guild for leading the nation in the Tide for Toys drive in 1950–51. Drew Pearson mentioned the award in his newspaper column.

A shooting war was not long in coming, however. By 1952, when General Dwight D. Eisenhower was elected President, the Korean conflict had grown from a "police action" into a full-fledged war. How costly was it? There were 54,426 American troops killed in Korea in three years, slightly fewer than the number who died in Vietnam over ten years. The war also produced 2 1/2 times the MIAs that Vietnam did and three times the POWs. Pennsylvania contributed more than its share of combatants, as usual, but the veterans of Korea were a largely forgotten group. The Pennsylvania department fought for their inclusion into Legion ranks. At post meetings throughout the state, veterans of World War II got to know newcomers who had returned from Korea. After pressure from the Legion's Legislative Committee, a "Korean War bill of rights" was drawn up. By 1955, in ten years, the Legion had become a united front of veterans of three major wars. The actions of Leesport Post #906 were typical of the department's efforts. In the summer of 1954, it held a testimonial dinner for thirty-five Korean veterans in which they were honored "as veterans of a noble fight" and invited to join the post as "members of a vigorous and enduring" organization.

By the spring of 1953, the average age of a Keystone veteran, like elsewhere in the United States, was about thirty-eight. The largest group was between thirty and thirty-four. The next group was between twenty-five and twenty-nine. As men with new families and other concerns, it was more difficult to recruit members by focusing exclusively on fellowship with other veterans. Instead, Legion programs emphasized service to the family, community, and nation. Legion baseball and other youth activities flourished as the "baby boom" flourished. It was no accident that Pennsylvania Legionnaires led other voluntary organizations in the number of good citizenship and community service awards granted by the United Way in the Fifties. In the meantime, the pressures of the Cold War created new concerns for America's premier veterans' organization.

Since 1919, the Legion had led the fight against Soviet-inspired Communism. The falling of the "Iron Curtain" in Eastern Europe, the rise of Red China, and the fear of Soviet-controlled espionage created serious concern among most Americans about the nation's security and internal strength. Once portrayed as extremist, the Legion now led "the vital center" of American society in the fight against totalitarianism. Like other departments, Pennsylvania worked with the House Un-American Activities Committee, supported anti-subversive campaigns in their communities, and supported the McCarran Act, which called for the registration of all members of the Communist Party and their incarceration in time of war or national crisis.

The Legion's Americanism program, the tenet of its philosophy, was again called into action. A newer feature was the emphasis on religion and religious instruction. As young and older family men, Legionnaires joined others in putting religious values back into the mainstream of American life. The Back to God campaign, begun by the Legion in conjunction with local and national religious groups, attempted to preserve religious expression in Europe and the United States. Radio "simulcasts" from New York and Washington featured speakers such as Eisenhower, Billy Graham, and Archbishop Fulton Sheen. State meetings followed this example. A fall meeting in 1952 was typical of gatherings organized by the campaign. Rabbis, ministers, and priests joined with Legion, Rotary, and Kiwanis members to discuss how religious values could be promoted. Herbert M. Walker, the principal speaker and Pennsylvania department commander, told the assembly, "One of my main objectives is the Back to God movement of the American Legion. This program will do more good for our country and for the world than any other program. We in Pennsylvania [are] leading this movement. . . . Communism has only one enemy, and that is Christianity." Later, this approach was amended to refer to the Judeo-Christian tradition in an effort to be as inclusive as possible.

The Legion's religious campaign emphasized what Americans held in common, not what separated them. When a Wisconsin Legionnaire published a letter in the *American Legion Maga-*

zine openly critical of Catholicism, the leadership of the Pennsylvania department jointly condemned him. "The American Legion," the statement read, "should not tolerate the presence of this man in its ranks for a single moment. His letter is the ravings of a maniac and he should be expelled from the Legion immediately."

Another example of the program was the Wooden Church Crusade to the war-devastated nations of Europe. Simply, the Legion proposed to rebuild churches and synagogues with American charitable donations. In 1953, for example, the campaign was organized to restore or replace the religious buildings of West Germany before Christmas. The Wooden Church Crusade asked all department and post chaplains to organize fund-raising campaigns. In keeping with the program's interdenominational character, Robert Jackson Legion Post #999 of Darby sent a contribution for $30, "designating that $10 was to be apportioned to a church or synagogue of each of the three faiths." Other posts in the state held dinners, auctions, raffles, and other events to raise funds. Religious films such as "Miracle at Fatima" were shown to emphasize the triumph of faith and the human spirit over totalitarianism. At the Cambria County War Memorial arena, more than 13,000 people watched this film during a five-day stretch sponsored by Johnstown Post #294.

The Americanism program also sought to get out the vote. The Keystone Legion, following national policy, applied the campaign to all voting, not just national elections. "Government has so completely permeated our lives," maintained Charles C. Miller, the state chairman of the 1954 campaign, "that every election is part of the big picture we call government." Americans too often wanted "good government" without devoting any time or energy to the practice of democracy, he said. "Register and vote at every election if you want good government and good public officials," Miller repeated during the campaign. During primary and general elections in 1954, Legionnaires throughout the state served as precinct captains and on election committees.

Americanism was demonstrated most vividly in the Keystone Legion's more innovative approaches to education. Legion posts throughout the country on May Day (May 1) 1955 staged mock

Communist takeovers of selected small towns. The Burt J. Asper Post #46 of Chambersburg organized an event in which the mayor was jailed, civil liberties suspended, and churches and synagogues closed. These and other examples of misrule were offered by Legionnaires, carrying dummy rifles and wearing red armbands. The mayor and other leading people were then subjected to a "show trial" in which they were sentenced to a "re-education camp." The day ended with a march to the public library and a "book burning" of various titles and magazines judged subversive by a "people's tribunal." The twenty-four-hour experiment with Stalin, as a local source described it, "taught the citizens of Chambersburg a vivid lesson in the brutalities to which people behind the Iron Curtain were subjected every day."

While the Cold War raged, a quieter battle was fought on behalf of the nation's veterans: the struggle to keep intact hospital service and the VA hospital system. The so-called Hoover Commission served as a clearinghouse for criticism of veterans' benefits and the VA. Created by President Eisenhower and headed by former president Herbert Hoover, this investigative body's task was to eliminate waste and fraud in government. It specifically requested the consolidation of the Veterans Administration with other federal agencies and the phased elimination of veterans' benefits over several decades. State departments had to publicize the fight for veterans' rights. Commander Herbert M. Walker led in the fight for the preservation of VA hospitals: "It is getting more and more difficult to get a sick and disabled veteran into a VA hospital. . . . There are today more than 10,000 empty beds in VA hospitals because money is lacking to operate them at a time when 30,000 sick and disabled veterans throughout the country are on the hospital waiting list."

The chief opponent of the VA remained the American Medical Association. It waged an unrelenting fight to cut back the amount—and perhaps the quality—of care for veterans. One resolution stated that a million more men were eligible every year for veterans' benefits. If this continued, the VA would soon "embrace the entire male population of the nation, making all eligible for free medical care in government hospitals, and thus lead to socialized medicine." The AMA proposed that medical care for veterans be turned over to community hospitals. Through this campaign, the AMA was an organizational spokesman for the pro-posals of the Hoover Commission. Spokesmen for the Keystone Legion were always ready to take on the proposals of the Hoover Commission. More often than not, Legion spokesmen and AMA officials were at loggerheads in the intermittent debates spon-sored by local civic groups. These forums often had statewide audiences, since many were broadcast.

Leaders of the Keystone Legion were usually on the front line in the struggle for veterans' rights at this time. Walker, the department commander in 1952, was a typical postwar Legion leader. A retired textile manufacturer, he devoted much of his time and fortune to Legion work. He was chairman of the Scot-land School Committee. At the 35th annual Legion convention in 1953, Walker followed Vincent A. Carroll and Walter Allesan-droni, both of Philadelphia, in being elected national vice com-mander. Throughout his career in the Legion, Walker campaigned to keep the VA system intact. This conflict over the "hearts and minds" of Americans was carried on wherever and whenever there was an audience.

Two incidents highlighted this issue. In the fall of 1953, department Commander Paul R. Selecky engaged the Hoover Commission supporters in debates and speeches. Calling the AMA's position untenable and absurd, he charged that a top-level clique in the association was opposed to hospital care "for the broken and sick veterans." Selecky "persuasively engaged" the audience, as a Pittsburgh newspaper noted, "using skill and logic" to show that the veteran population would soon level off and that needs could be met without wrecking the federal bud-get. Selecky defined the issue as one of obligation, not entitle-ment. "If our government sees fit to place us in a special class to fight for our land, why shouldn't that nation place us in a special class in combatting the ravages of war?" he asked.

Soon after, a 1954 debate in Philadelphia between Joseph A.C. Girone, state Legion parliamentarian, and Dr. Edward Hanna, an AMA supporter, was carried over radio station WPEN. Hanna said veterans considered themselves to be a special class. Girone noted an attempt by the AMA to get a special tax exemp-tion for its members as well as a $100-a-month pay increase for military doctors. Among more than 100 public opinion mea-sures, a telephone poll was taken after the two-hour debate;

respondents were divided into those who had no veterans in the family and those with veterans as immediate relations. In the first category "the vote was 10–10." To break the tie, additional voters were polled, and the total was 14–11 against the American Legion's position. In the second category the vote favored the American Legion by a margin of 14–6. The overall vote favored the American Legion by a score of 25–10.

Faced with the ebbing membership many voluntary organizations were experiencing because of a new competition—television—and the dislocation that accompanied the exodus to the suburbs, the Keystone Legion determined to preserve its membership. In 1954, the department created a division to boost the annual membership roundup scheduled in the fall. The theme was "Knock on Every Door in '54." Alex Viggiano of Pittsburgh and Lawrenceville Post #531 were chosen to head this effort. The department also worked tirelessly to boost the circulation of its monthly newspaper, the *Pennsylvania Legionnaire,* which in the Fifties was sent to only 5,000 of Pennsylvania's 275,000 Legionnaires. Through community programs as diverse as blood drives and Memorial Day parades, Legion posts across the state kept alive the spirit of the Legion's founders. The years ahead would see further tests of the Legion's vision, relevance, and strength of purpose.

Pennsylvanian Eric Fisher Wood played a pivotal role in the formation of the American Legion and worked tirelessly to recruit veterans to the new organization.

Franklin D'Olier, a Philadelphia textile manufacturer who later founded Prudential Insurance, was elected national commander at the Legion's first convention in Minneapolis in 1919.

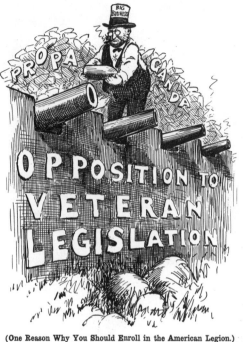

BEHLER-HEIN POST NO. 637
AMERICAN LEGION
HAMBURG, - - - *PENNSYLVANIA*

(One Reason Why You Should Enroll in the American Legion.)

This pamphlet, circulated in 1919, illustrates the prominent role veterans' issues have played in Legion recruiting efforts.

The Legion's organization proceeded rapidly in Pennsylvania. William Murdock of Milton presided over the first statewide meeting of Legionnaires, held in Harrisburg on October 24, 1919.

The Legion Parade was an important feature of the Department Convention in Pittsburgh in September 1921.

Parades were also highlights of the national conventions, such as the one held in Philadelphia in October 1926.

At the time it was built, the York Legion Post #127 was valued at $100,000.

Housed in the historic Girard Bank on Third Street in Philadelphia, the department headquarters included the Adjutant's Office, the Office of Child Welfare Department, and (shown here) the Headquarters Office.

This publication was produced by Yeoman F Post #50 of Philadelphia, one of several all-female posts of the Pennsylvania Legion.

THE PROPELLER

AMERICAN·LEGION·YEOMEN·F·POST·50.

Vol. XIV MAY, 1936 No. 14

Second Annual HISTORY FILE
Americanization Rally

auspices of

THIRTY-FOURTH DISTRICT

AMERICAN LEGION

DEPARTMENT OF PENNSYLVANIA

in participation with

The Federal Bureau of
Immigration and Naturalization

Soldiers' & Sailors'
Memorial Hall

Fifth Avenue and Bigelow Boulevard, Pittsburgh, Pa.

Wednesday, May 1, 1940, at 8:00 P. M.

HEAR
LOUIS A. JOHNSON
Assistant Secretary of War

This is the most impressive exposition of Americanism held in the Country!

Bring Your Friends!

The Keystone Legion fostered Americanism through a number of means, including rallies and educational programs.

ALTOONA

AUGUST 14-15-16 · 1941

AMERICAN LEGION STATE CONVENTION

Drum and Bugle Corps
State Championship Contest

FRIDAY, AUGUST 15th

A deluge of requests for reservations at Altoona's great Mansion Park Stadium to witness the spectacular Drum and Bugle Corps competition, August 15, is pouring in to the committee in charge.

Mansion Park Football Stadium, which has one of the finest turf fields in the east, has a seating capacity of 18,000, but the supply of reserved seats is limited, so send in your reservation N O W. Price for reserved seats is $3.00.

This beautiful Altoona stadium is being equipped with the latest floodlighting units so that the thousands of spectators will be enabled to see clearly all details of the precision maneuvers of the

75 to 100 brilliantly uniformed corps expected to participate.

Miss Gladys Holsinger, winner of the national Majorette contest and best baton twirler at the A. A. Patrol Boys' convention in Washington, D. C., this Spring, will welcome visiting Drum Majorettes as Blair County's Official Drum Majorette Hostess.

This year's convention Drum and Bugle Corps competition will be one of the most thrilling presentations of martial pageantry in State Department history. It will be one of the big highlights of a sparkling and busy program for the 1941 convention in Altoona.

DON'T MISS IT!

PRIZES $4,000
ALSO GOLF, SWIMMING

Drum and bugle corps competitions and participant sports were standard events at annual state conventions.

The 1943 state convention in Wilkes-Barre was billed as "no frills, no thrills . . . business only" and emphasized the need to sacrifice for the war effort.

Streamlined War Year Convention!   Buy Bonds Help Build Morale!

WILKES-BARRE
AUGUST 12, 13, 14, 1943
American Legion 25th Annual State Convention

No Parades
No Frills
No Thrills

No Drum Corps
or Bands . . .
Business Only

HOUSING INFORMATION—For Delegates Only

Apply for your reservations NOW! Don't delay! Choice rooms go first. All assignments made in the order received.

Reservations at hotels for full convention period. (Wednesday Noon Aug. 10th to Saturday 6:00 P. M. Aug. 14th.)

Assignment will be made only on receipt of your remittance in full.

Therefore, send us, as early as possible, information concerning reservations necessary for delegates only.

HOTEL RATES
$1.50
TO
$3.50
Per Day Per Person 2 or More to the Room

HEADQUARTERS: STERLING HOTEL

REDINGTON, AMERICAN LEGION AUXILIARY HEADQUARTERS

Complete information will avoid unnecessary correspondence. Kindly furnish the names and number in your party.

For reservations and information, address
AMERICAN LEGION CONVENTION CORP.
Hotel Sterling, Wilkes-Barre, Pa.

★ ★ ★ THIS IS AMERICA AT WAR ★ ★ ★

Rising through the Legion ranks, Paul Griffith of Uniontown was elected department commander in 1932; he helped write the Four-Point Program, which restored benefits to thousands of disabled veterans. He went on to serve as national commander in 1946.

Legionnaire President Harry S. Truman spoke at the opening session of the 31st national convention of the American Legion in Philadelphia on August 29, 1949.

Shamokin's Lincoln Post #73, one of the most impressive post buildings in the department, was dedicated on November 11, 1924, to the members of the Armed Forces who took part in the Great War of 1917–18.

Several Veterans Administration hospitals were closed in the mid-60s because of government budget cuts; this one in Wilkes-Barre remains open to provide healthcare to area veterans.

Past National Commander Paul Griffith from Uniontown (standing) helped organize against Veterans Administration hospital closings. Working with him was National Executive Committeeman Daniel A. Drew of Pittsburgh.

Upon his return from France in 1919, Edward A. Linsky joined the American Legion and helped organize the William T. Shetzline Post #96. He served the Legion in a number of capacities and was appointed department adjutant in 1935.

At the 1958 national convention in Chicago, this Pennsylvania contingent of the "Forty and Eight" lived up to the society's reputation for fun-making.

Active in Legion activities as a boy, Edward T. Hoak of Manor joined the Legion after military service and was later elected department commander at the age of 36. He served as department adjutant from 1963 until 1991.

National Commander Eldon James spoke at an October 1965 "Freedom Is Not Free" Rally held on the steps of the state capitol in support of all those serving in Vietnam.

Auxiliary Department President Mary Fisher presented a poppy to Governor William Scranton during the 1966 poppy campaign. Also pictured are Department Commander Harry Klein with his daughter Mary Beth and then-Attorney General Walter Alessandroni.

The department head-
quarters were located for
a time on Front Street in
Harrisburg in the former
Stackpole Mansion.

The "father" of Legion
baseball, George E. Bellis
guided Pennsylvania's
program for thirty-one
years. Among the one
hundred boys he saw reach
the majors were Stan Musial
and Roy Campanella.

The department headquarters building in Wormleysburg, shown here in an artist's sketch, was dedicated on April 26, 1970.

In 1980, E. Thomas Cammarota, past department commander and national committeeman, announced his candidacy for national commander, challenging the national organization's practice of presenting one generally unopposed candidate each year.

POW★MIA

H.F.
Pennsylvania
Dept.
Convention
1983

65th ANNUAL CONVENTION
DEPARTMENT OF PENNSYLVANIA
THE AMERICAN LEGION

JULY 13, 14, 15, 16, 1983   PITTSBURGH, PA

US
AMERICAN LEGION

COMMITTEES
MEMBERSHIP

FINANCES
HOSPITAL

REPORT OF OFFICERS
AMENDMENT PROPOSALS

The issue of prisoners of war and those missing in action has been addressed constantly by the Pennsylvania Legion and was the theme of the 1983 convention.

Pennsylvania Legionnaires participated in the dedication ceremonies for the Vietnam War Memorial in Washington, D.C.

In 1991, Dominic D. diFrancesco of Middletown become the third Pennsylvanian to be named national commander.

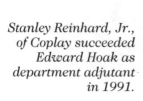

Stanley Reinhard, Jr., of Coplay succeeded Edward Hoak as department adjutant in 1991.

CHAPTER

5

REMAINING RELEVANT
The Keystone Legion,
1954–76

T he years between Korea and Vietnam saw both continuity and change in the Pennsylvania Legion. Commanders came and went, conventions were held every summer, and posts went about their business. At the same time, there were massive changes in culture and society. The Vietnam War forced the Legion to take controversial but consistent stands in defense of the nation.

The annual convention remained the focus of activity for the average Pennsylvania Legionnaire. The 36th meeting of the department convened in Philadelphia from July 22–24, 1954. About 90,000 delegates and their families deliberated resolutions, renewed acquaintances, and underscored the importance of fighting the Cold War, maintaining veterans' benefits, and keeping up membership.

During this time, Legion posts sponsored everything from athletics to stamp-collecting clubs for all ages. Even more, the Legion paved the way for membership for Korea veterans. Several recently discharged men spoke at the 1954 convention, and resolutions were framed with their concerns in mind. Resolution #188 was unanimously approved; it endorsed a state Bonus for Korea vets. The issue dominated the legislative agenda of the Pennsylvania Legion for the next three years.

As it was during the interwar years, it wasn't easy getting the Bonus for Korean War veterans. They made up a smaller proportion of the population than did veterans of either world war. For the Keystone Legion, however, the Bonus was a matter of justice and self-interest. Those who served in Korea had equally put their lives on the line and were entitled to the same benefits. The Korean War created nearly 40,000 prospective Legionnaires in Pennsylvania, and those who had already joined almost immediately demanded the same as what their predecessors had received. The Legion spearheaded the drive to put the Bonus for Korea veterans to a referendum, and thousands of Legionnaires lobbied for it in their communities.

The Bonus bill was approved resoundingly in the November 5, 1957, general election. It allowed the state to borrow up to $150 million to pay Korean War veterans a cash bonus. Pennsylvania was already among the twenty-one states that paid a bonus to World War II veterans, and the new law put it among fifteen to pay a bonus to Korea veterans. The benefit was to be $10 a month for those who served in the armed forces between June 25, 1950, and July 27, 1953. If the veteran had died while in service, a flat $500 was to be paid to survivors.

The new Bonus was the culmination of several years of work by the Keystone Legion. The department commander in 1957–58, John W. Collins, noted that in the referendum campaign, "veterans' organizations in Pennsylvania completely vindicated themselves [of criticism that they had no interest in the Korean War veteran] and . . . the veterans [of both world wars] can be proud of their deep concern for their buddies who also served in this tough but unusual war." Collins also reminded veterans that they would have to wait at least a year before receiving any payments. The vote only paved the way for the Legislature to decide upon a tax program to repay the $150 mil-

lion. "It is going to be a tough assignment for the legion to get a
. . . response from the legislators."

How the Bonus was to be paid became controversial. Supporters wished to make the financing as painless as possible to
Pennsylvanians; opponents wished to tie it up with even more
controversial legislation. The Legion's Bonus Committee walked
a thin line between support for the Bonus and averting the ire of
any other special-interest group. A sales tax was regressive; an
income tax would possibly hurt business and employment. A
compromise was reached to pay off the long-term loan taken out
to cover the Bonus.

Pennsylvania's Korean War veterans, Legionnaires or not,
were fortunate to have Collins as department commander. His
Legion service began twelve years earlier at the Milton L. Bishop
Post #301 in Connelsville. Before joining, he had served with the
1st Division in the Normandy, Rhineland, and Ardennes campaigns, earning the Bronze Star and European Theater Medal
with five stars. He was elected post commander in 1947. In suc-
ceeding years, he served as western vice commander, with
simultaneous recognition as department senior vice commander
in charge of membership. Collins also was appointed to the Connelsville Housing Authority and was the town's first civil defense
director following World War II. He was particularly adroit in
gaining financing of the Korean War Bonus.

The Bonus campaign could not have succeeded if the image
of the Legion had not been high in the state. In the mid-1950s,
in fact, the American Legion enjoyed the highest popularity of
any private group or voluntary organization. In a national
Roper poll taken at the time, it was found to have a greater
favorability rating than most private groups and organizations.
The department commander for 1955–56, Sherman W. Mason,
said, "We believe we enjoy this prestige with the citizens of our
nation because we have never abused the power to speak for
our 3,000,000 members." Like the national organization, the
Keystone Legion could keep the support of veterans only if it
heeded their concerns.

Potential members wanted to know about the advantages of
belonging to the Legion. Local campaigns stressed the fact that
men of substance and recognition continued to join the local
posts. Men of national recognition also could be counted as

members. In 1955, a membership campaign coordinator said, "The American Legion has more members of a variety of occupations than any other organization." He also pointed out that President Eisenhower, fifty-nine Senators, and thirty-three governors were Legionnaires. "Right now, the Legion needs the strength of membership to back a continuing fight" to maintain benefits.

The power of the Pennsylvania Legion was in sheer numbers. Though the state's population declined in these years, Legion membership remained comparatively high. In 1956, six Pennsylvania posts were among the biggest in the nation. Gen. David M. Gregg Post #12 of Reading was the largest with 3,684 members and Harrisburg Post #27 was second with 3,263. They were followed by East Liberty Post #5 of Pittsburgh, Wilkes-Barre Post #132, Koch-Conley Post #121 of Scranton, and William H. Nauss Post #143 of New Cumberland. By 1957, more than 1,786,000 veterans had joined, according to membership director Richard Viggiano.

The size and influence of the Pennsylvania Legion in the mid-Fifties was reflected in the rapid rise of certain Pennsylvanians to national leadership. John F. Stay, a Quaker Oats sales executive in Philadelphia, was elected national vice commander in 1956 following a rapid rise through the Pennsylvania department. After his discharge from the Navy in 1945, Stay joined the Russell H. Conwell Post #264 and held many offices in the Philadelphia County Legion organization. In 1950, he was the first World War II veteran to be elected commander of his district. He was department vice commander in 1952–53; served on many committees, including the department Executive Committee; and he was Pennsylvania commander in 1955–56. Whether he was in office or simply "among the guys" in his post, Stay has been a strength for decades in the Keystone Legion.

Much of the controversy surrounding the Keystone Legion at this time stemmed from anti-radical activities. Legionnaires professed the dangers of Communism and its agents in the United States, along with members of organized labor, the business community, and the entertainment industry. All participated in the anti-Communist campaigns of the era. Since the

Legion stood for "100 percent Americanism" and the principles of a free society, it was only logical that it take the lead.

Most of the Keystone Legion's work was educational. Posts sponsored pro-American rallies, held forums on life behind the Iron Curtain, and worked to expose Communist operations. Legion pressure helped to ban Charlie Chaplin films at Muhlenberg College. The Legion felt that Chaplin, an open critic of American life, should not be subsidized by American customers. Heeding a protest from an Allentown post, the college president canceled a Chaplin festival. The Keystone Legion also fought for the reversal of a State Supreme Court ruling that freed Steve Nelson, an avowed leader of the Communist Party, from prison on the ground that a 1919 sedition law was invalid. In the Pittsburgh area, Legion trade unionists worked to isolate and expel Communists who tried to conduct subversive activities under the guise of the peace movement.

Americanism meant not just anti-Communism but an affirmation of civil rights and responsibilities. The Pennsylvania Legion also worked to preserve the quality of education. In 1955, Commander Sherman W. Mason took up the cause of schoolteachers "because deterioration of the public school system puts the future of the nation in jeopardy." Proper patriotic instruction was "a capital investment in the future."

The fight against Communism took an occasional humorous and ironic twist. State Legionnaires were asked to contact their congressmen urging the passage of a bill requiring that "In God We Trust" be inscribed on U.S. currency. John H. Shenkel, Americanism chairman of Allegheny County, said, "The sooner we get this bill into effect, the quicker we will convey to the world a true picture of what the United States stands for. Our paper money is used by Communists and the inscription 'In God We Trust' will make every Communist an agent to spread the word of 'God.' "

The Legion's work after the Korean War maintained a spiritual theme, with no favoritism toward any faith. The 1958 religious emphasis program of Media's Smith-Howard Post #93 typified the Legion's approach and style: "For a number of years, our post has distributed the grace-before-meal cards and the traveler's prayer cards in restaurants and gas stations in Media just prior to Good Friday. . . . [W]e would like to mention the fact that Roman Catholics, Protestants of all denominations, Jews, colored and white made this program possible, thus exemplifying the ideals of Americanism and the American Legion."

The Keystone Legion also fought for the rights of recently discharged servicemen. One celebrated case involved a Pennsylvania veteran who had been charged with a crime in Korea. In the autumn of 1955, the state Legion successfully barred prosecution of discharged servicemen by military authorities. Robert W. Toth of Pittsburgh had been accused of murdering a Korean civilian while in service. The twenty-four-year-old Toth was arrested by military police on May 13, 1953, five months after his discharge. He was then flown back to Korea to stand trial. At the time, Toth was working in a steel mill in Pittsburgh. The Keystone Legion provided legal counsel, organized meetings and demonstrations, and supplied constant support to Toth and his family during this ordeal, which lasted several years.

The Keystone Legion was still quick to respond to local emergencies. In the late 1950s, Stroudsburg was devastated in a flood that left sixty-four people dead, sixty-two homes demolished, and many businesses and industrial plants destroyed. Members of the George N. Kemp Post #346 manned boats to rescue trapped victims, directed traffic, and organized and staffed relief centers. Within days, truckloads of clothing, food, and furniture began arriving in Stroudsburg from posts throughout the state and other departments. Cash was collected by mail through the department headquarters. The junior baseball tournament in Allentown contributed $268 to the relief fund. One local member of the Chamber of Commerce suggested, "The local American Legion has not just shown the way in rebuilding Stroudsburg; it has demonstrated a sense of sacrifice and fellowship unseen in many years."

As always, the Executive Committee acted as a steering mechanism for the Keystone Legion. In Pittsburgh on March 7, 1959, it met to discuss current and potential challenges. The Bonus for Korean War veterans was discussed in the context of the governor's financing plan. Also, Frank Berman, director of Americanism activities, stated: "I am greatly disappointed at the small number of Legion posts who have requested my services. . . . so I say that we've got to beat the drum, wave the flag, and speak on

Americanism for the American Legion every single minute of the day." The committee also commented upon the lagging energy of the rank and file. A survey of the national organization revealed that fewer than 10 percent of the members were carrying the workload for the 3 million-member organization. In turn, there were 18 million veterans who enjoyed benefits secured by the Legion but "who were not interested enough to belong." Increasingly, veterans, whether they were Legionnaires or not, were content to "let George do it."

"The Legion post is too often seen as just another watering hole," one committeeman lamented in 1962, "with the average Legionnaire knowing little and caring less about the ideals that lie behind the organization." Rural posts, especially those dominated by World War I veterans, let their charters expire or merged with other posts. Pennsylvania posts, however, continued to lead the nation in Americanism activities. From 1956–64, the Pennsylvania department received the national organization's Americanism award. Before that, Pennsylvania was given the award for eighteen of the twenty-six years of the trophy's existence. The honor was based on the percentage of posts conducting each Americanism activity listed in the annual report form submitted by posts to the department. Pennsylvania posts led or were close to the lead in the sponsorship of school awards, flag education, baseball teams, and Boy Scout troops from 1954–76.

The Pennsylvania department was not afraid of controversy. In April 1963, the Executive Committee was asked by several posts in Philadelphia and Pittsburgh to confront segregation in the Legion. After a lengthy meeting, it passed a resolution protesting the segregation laws that were to be enforced in New Orleans during the Legion's national convention in September. Department Commander Louis J. Greco urged that the convention be moved if "the present segregation laws enforced will deny housing and eating facilities to all Legionnaires and Auxiliary members because of their race." Letters of protest were mailed to all departments and their adjutants, as well as national Commander Powers and members of the national Executive Committee. The national officers were asked to demand that changes be enacted or the site of the upcoming convention be moved. This change reflected the energy of the new department adjutant. Edward T. Hoak epitomized the second generation of veterans who had joined the Legion after World War II. He had more than twenty-eight years of experience with the Legion. As a boy, he was active in Legion youth activities, earning a school award in 1937. After military service, he joined the Carl Leroy McKelvey Post #472 of Manor and held every office there. Hoak was distinguished by being elected department commander at age thirty-six. Since the early 1970s, Hoak had tried to assert the Pennsylvania department's strength by running for national commander. He wished to be the first Pennsylvanian since 1946 to attain this position. Hoak's quiet demeanor belied his experience and inner strength; people were often surprised to learn that he had been a baton-swinging military policeman and had served in the United Nations honor guard.

The 46th department convention, held in Philadelphia from July 15–18, 1964, was typical of the assemblies of the 1960s. About 225,000 Pennsylvania Legionnaires acted on sixty-six resolutions. Mayor James H. Tate welcomed the Legionnaires and General Mark W. Clark was a featured speaker. Monroe Bethman of Doylestown was elected commander and David Minto of Trafford, Robert Ertwine of Ringtown, and Hugh Cunningham of Blossburg were elected vice commanders. The closing parade had 10,000 marchers.

Former department Commander Paul Griffith opened the four-day 1964 department convention with a memorable speech. The former national commander had recently toured the Soviet Union with a delegation of current and former State Department officials. He told the Legionnaires that "Communism is a cancerous philosophy which hasn't worked in Russia and will not work anywhere else in the world." Griffith said his recent trip "made him all the more certain" of Communist failure "and strengthened his faith in the American system." He told the Russians whom he met that they mistakenly believe American prosperity was founded on a war economy "and that consequently the people of the United States favor heavy arms production." In numerous discussions he had with Soviet citizens, he argued convincingly both of the peaceful nature of the United States and that the American economy produced "more and more goods and services, not just instruments of death."

One of the most representative of the state Legion leaders at this time was the department commander for 1964–65, Monroe R. Bethman. "Monty" began his Legion career after World War II, when he joined the Albert R. Atkinson Post #210 in Doylestown. Drafted in 1941, Bethman entered the chemical warfare branch of the Army and gained a commission. He saw action in the South Pacific and served in the United States with various civilian aid projects.

After the war, Bethman returned to Doylestown and, with the help of a $5,000 GI loan, started a heating oil business. It grew and soon operated out of a huge plant north of Doylestown, thanks to hard work and contacts developed through Legion activities. As his post's activities director, commander, and head of various department offices, Bethman learned the ins and outs of the Keystone Legion in the Fifties, most significantly as a member of the national Security Commission. He was unanimously elected department commander at the state convention in Philadelphia. Leadership was "not a new experience for him," but he was surprised by the extent of the detail and legwork involved in his duties. His work took him over 20,000 miles after his election. "They [the Legion] take good care of me," Bethman said to a Pittsburgh reporter. "I get travel allowances and subsistence pay while on the road or on Legion business." His daily schedule was "filled with meetings, lunch, dinner, and more meetings, all in different Pennsylvania towns." Many of the communities Bethman visited he had "never even heard of" before his tour as department commander. Bethman worked hard to improve the image of the Legion in his state. "Too many times," he stated, "it's just a social group that takes on one or two social projects a year and nothing the rest of the year." The department commander spent much of his time encouraging both the small and the "larger, inactive posts" to "get on their feet and accomplish something." In a short time, the 47-year-old bachelor had become known throughout the state as the hardest-working Legionnaire. Until his death in a house fire in 1968, Bethman sought to preserve the Pennsylvania Legion as a responsive and civic-minded organization.

More often than not, however, Bethman was happy to discover Legion posts of all sizes involved in many activities. He prized Americanism work. In an interview in the *Philadelphia Inquirer,* he defended the Legion's record of patriotic service. Legionnaires were active in Americanism programs for the schools, charity drives, and youth activities. "So many times, you can see part of the Legion using it as a Red-baiting tactic, but in my way of thinking, it's just a positive approach, putting America first," he said.

The most significant development in the mid-Sixties was the Veterans Administration decision to close eleven hospitals, four domiciliary homes, and sixteen regional offices. The sudden announcement was stunning and "revealed a situation in which the congressional forces were without power to act," according to the department adjutant's newsletter to post commanders. The executive power of the president, with this unilateral decision by the Johnson administration, was disclosed for the first time since the Depression.

Bethman and his officers became immediately involved in the attempted closing of the VA facility at Wilkes-Barre. He led a delegation of state Legionnaires and Wilkes-Barre VA officials to Washington to plead the case of disabled and needy veterans. The department commander persuaded twenty-four of the state's twenty-seven congressmen to attend a midweek meeting in the House Foreign Affairs Committee room at the Capitol. "Veterans have a right, an earned right, to healthcare," stated Bethman at a press conference. Daniel J. Flood told Legionnaires that the villain in the story of the VA closings was the Bureau of the Budget. He said that if the closings were to be averted, "the order would have to come from the White House." The Dean of the state's congressional caucus, Dr. Thomas E. Morgan, was instrumental in getting a hearing before the House Veterans Affairs Committee.

Later in the day, the Pennsylvania Legionnaires met with the new VA administrator, William J. Driver, and gave him 637 petitions bearing 60,000 signatures protesting the proposed closings. Appearing with Bethman were several past department commanders and department adjutant Ed Hoak. Others present included the mayor of Scranton and officials from Luzerne County. Bethman later noted that "We gave Mr. Driver [the] facts and proof why the Wilkes-Barre office should remain open." He and the others argued the case that the "Veterans

Administration just can't ignore the fact that the Wilkes-Barre office was judged the best office for three years, and is now subject to being closed."

These actions persuaded the administration to reconsider the decision. Johnson appointed a committee to study the situation, and the immediate closing of the facility was thus postponed, this by the quick action of the Legion. The facility was ultimately saved from budget cuts.

Legion posts in several parts of the state also started joint campaigns to spur economic growth. Throughout the post-World War II era, Pennsylvania endured higher unemployment than the rest of the nation; in western Pennsylvania, the percentage of unemployed was 10 to 15 percent greater than in the rest of the state. Forty-five percent of the unemployed in the steel and anthracite coal industries were veterans of either the Second World War or Korea. The Pennsylvania department sought to bring industry, government, and labor together to solve these problems. For example, Dr. Almo J. Sebastianelli of Jessup, commander of District 11, worked with the Scranton Chamber of Commerce to obtain federal aid to ease growing unemployment in northeastern Pennsylvania. Both organizations were concerned with the lack of opportunity in the area, which compelled people to move to greener pastures. They especially wanted to channel defense work to industries in the area. Sebastianelli said, "As men and women who fought wars to preserve the American way of life, we know too well that sound economy is fundamental to the preservation of the happy home." Legionnaires, he said, sought "no charity—they want jobs, they want and deserve the opportunity to work . . . and they will be more than willing to go out and push for the opportunity to work and earn."

The Keystone Legion was one of the first to press for the admittance of new veterans. A special report compiled by the Pennsylvania department and submitted to the national Executive Committee asked whether "the American Legion should change its eligibility requirements to admit veterans of current military actions." A special fact-finding committee was appointed by the national commander, largely through the lobbying of the Keystone Legion, and was to report to the upcoming 1965 national convention in Portland, Oregon.

The escalation of the Vietnam War created great controversy among Americans. Following the lead of the national organization, the Keystone Legion organized events to promote support for servicemen and the cause for which they fought. Semi-regular patriotic rallies were held in 1965–66 on the state capitol steps, featuring speakers from the national organization; state officials, such as Lieutenant Governor Raymond Shafer; and the department commander. These events regularly drew large crowds and outnumbered anti-war rallies that were often more prominently seen in the news.

The committee noted that the American Legion had been organized in 1919 and reorganized in 1942 to limit its membership to men and women who had served during a period of "actual hostilities." Another change in eligibility was made to accommodate Korea veterans, who served during an undeclared war.

The committee, of which Walter Alessandroni and Ed Hoak were members, noted that combat conditions then existed in Vietnam, but there had been no declaration of war nor designation of a national emergency. The committee concluded that if a change were made, August 5, 1964, should be the date for opening eligibility. This was the date of U.S. retaliation against enemy ships in the Gulf of Tonkin.

In his report, Hoak reminded national headquarters that, since 1958, there had been several deployments of American troops in several areas of hostilities (in Lebanon, Vietnam, Berlin, and Laos, for instance) and enclosed a copy of a letter from the late President Kennedy establishing the Armed Forces Expeditionary Medal. This was given to those who served in "hostile action" after July 1, 1958. If service in "flash points" of the Cold War was enough to receive a medal from the federal government, Hoak reasoned, it was enough for membership in the Legion. Despite the lobbying of Pennsylvania and like-minded departments, some in the national organization continued to insist, according to the *American Legion Magazine,* "that the Legion should retain its historical character," shutting out thousands of potential members. The issue was tabled for later consideration.

The tumult of the Sixties forced nearly every institution to change. The 49th convention of the Pennsylvania department saw a renewed commitment to activism. "Every effort will be expended to revitalize our organization's public image," pledged the new commander, Theodore F. Roedisch, a Philadelphia real estate man. The Keystone Legion sought to rebuild bridges between veterans and the community that had been damaged by dissent. This required a new organizational commitment and energy and was largely accomplished within twelve months in 1967–68.

In these months, there were a variety of changes. Final papers were signed for the purchase of land in Wormleysburg, where a new headquarters was to be constructed. The largest crowd ever attended the statewide membership drive held at Post #27 in Harrisburg. Work began on the fiftieth anniversary of the national organization. This coincided with publicity drives such as Operation Servicemen and Freedom Is Not Free, which provided much-needed reminders of the sacrifices of veterans. Legion posts throughout the late Sixties and early Seventies entertained and courted the opinion of Vietnam veterans in Pennsylvania. By the middle of 1968, membership in the Pennsylvania Legion hit 224,000, up 8,000 over the previous year. The state leadership also chartered four new posts and approved plans for five others.

The Keystone Legion also received overdue awards and citations. The Reverend Edward P. Nolan of Post #781 was elected national chaplain. Hoak received the Pennsylvania Police Chiefs award for his work with juveniles. The freighter *American Legion* was christened before a capacity crowd in Chester. Pennsylvania won the National Service Trophy for its welfare work for veterans and their dependents. These were typical of the awards won previously in the department's history.

The late Sixties also saw the formation of an advisory group composed of recently discharged servicemen to help formulate Keystone Legion policy on Vietnam veterans. "This is a crying need within the organization," one Legion officer told a Scranton paper. The support of these veterans was of special importance; the Pennsylvania delegation to the 1967 national convention in Boston included two Vietnam veterans, C. William Hill and John C. Kresovich, who were representatives to the Legion's Vietnam Advisory Committee.

A man of particular significance to the Keystone Legion was E. Thomas Cammarota, a plumbing contractor from South

Philadelphia who was elected department commander at the 52nd state convention in Harrisburg. The forty-seven-year-old combat Marine had been active in patriotic matters and veterans' issues. At eighteen, Cammarota enlisted in the Marine Corps and saw action on Guam, Bougainville, and Guadalcanal over four years. After his honorable discharge in 1945, Cammarota was active in a myriad of civic and voluntary organizations. It was in veterans' politics, however, that he attained prominence. In 1948, he joined the Marine Corps League and also was a member of the Veterans of Foreign Wars. The Legion, however, became Cammarota's second home and it was there that he did his most important work. In 1970, he helped organize the Rally for America in Philadelphia, which sponsored a parade marking the twenty-eighth anniversary of the attack on Pearl Harbor. In March 1969, he led a coalition of local veterans' groups that demanded that the University of Pennsylvania choose sides on whether to ban the radical Students for a Democratic Society. He later charged that a core of fifty-three faculty members was depriving the vast majority of students at the university of their rights by promoting radical activities. Cammarota argued that since the university received federal funds, it should be subject to sedition laws that had been on the books since the 1950s.

Obviously, the new state Legion commander was not shy about controversy. Even before Vietnam became divisive, Cammarota actively sought federal prosecution, on grounds of treason and sedition, of individuals who sent anti-war literature to servicemen in Southeast Asia. He actively protested against closings of national cemeteries to veterans of Vietnam and suggested legislation to regulate and license all "businesses selling goods made in Communist countries."

Cammarota had come into office with a goal and a method. From the start, his message—in the words of Toastmasters International—was: "There is no such thing as a generation gap and there never has been, but there *is* a communications gap." Cammarota sought to re-energize and enliven the Keystone Legion with novelty and innovation. He revived previous methods of recruitment and initiated new ones. A meeting of the department Executive Committee in January 1974 reflected the current issues. The two-day affair passed resolutions and debated policy that affected thousands of Legionnaires and other veterans in Pennsylvania. Two concerned the energy crisis: One, Cammarota's own, urged that fuel exports be banned and called for a commission to regulate energy prices; the other, submitted by Hoak, expressed the Pennsylvania Legion's opposition "to any trade agreements or commitments for the development of gas and oil in the U.S.S.R."

Other issues were debated that greatly affected the veterans of Pennsylvania. Participants urged the president and the Pennsylvania Legislature to comply with veterans' preference laws in civil service recruitment. They urged support for a House bill to give retired enlisted men the same method of computation of retirement pay as that enjoyed by officers. They suggested that a study be made of using Valley Forge Army Hospital, which had recently closed, as a nursing home for veterans. Other resolutions included one that urged workers and managers in state buildings to display the American flag. Another urged that "in view of attacks on policemen in large cities," two-man patrol cars be considered in Philadelphia and Pittsburgh.

The committee also heard from Joshua Eilberg, a congressman and Legionnaire from Philadelphia. He said, "If the bond which cements the American Legion were rooted only in past service, this organization would be weak indeed. Fortunately for American veterans as well as the rest of the citizenry, the American Legion is an active community organization with its roots firmly planted in the present and the future." The congressman reported on the status of veterans' legislation and stated, "It is becoming increasingly clear that some sort of pension reform is necessary," citing inequities among benefits to veterans and dependents. Eilberg noted that Hoak and the State Veterans' Commission had "always been of invaluable assistance to the Committee on Veterans' Affairs" and urged continued support, noting that veterans and their dependents and survivors represented nearly half of the population.

Expanding or at least maintaining membership increasingly preoccupied the Legion leadership. In 1974, though a number of districts improved on their standing, the state average increase stood at 72.5 percent against a 75 percent target. "Many of the districts have improved their position," Hoak said, not "because of their own efforts but because of even greater decreases on the part of districts which last year held top spots." The biggest district on January 5, for example, moved up from fourth place but showed an overall decrease of 134 members. "This is hardly an improvement," Hoak acknowledged. He also noted that a survey among all veterans in the state compared with Legion members revealed that the Keystone Legion was losing touch. Hoak was particularly concerned that fewer posts were community centers. "Too many of our members ask what they get from, not what they give to, the Legion and America at large."

Though Pennsylvania consistently had the largest department, it had not had a national commander since Paul H. Griffith in 1947. More than a few Legionnaires, inside and outside the state, felt that this was not coincidental. Pennsylvania had often led the way on controversial proposals. Hoak said of particular irritation was the issue of who initiated the membership change that allowed Vietnam veterans to join. He told a friend in the New York Legion, "The resolution that was adopted was the [one] I had written and circulated throughout the other departments, even though national [headquarters] got the credit for the change in eligibility." This dissatisfaction eventually spurred some department leaders to seek national office.

Hoak tried several times to shake up the hierarchy by putting his name in for nomination as national commander. In 1973, still as adjutant of the Pennsylvania department, he began a campaign for the national office, challenging Robert Eaton, a past Maryland department commander and a retired lieutenant general. Eaton was favored by the kingmakers within the organization, allegedly led by various state adjutants who had been in the Legion for decades. After a nearly two-month campaign that tested the waters, Hoak withdrew in May 1973. Though he conceded he was an underdog, Hoak said his independent candidacy had been gaining nationwide support, adding that the Legion needed vigorous campaigning until the reform movement succeeded.

Such campaigning carried risks. Hoak later said his candidacy had caused Pennsylvania to be penalized. At a press conference in early 1973, Hoak named some Pennsylvanians who had been recommended for appointments but were turned down. "These Legionnaires don't just fill chairs at committee meetings; these are distinguished Legionnaires that serve and have served this organization. . . . What a shame and disgrace to lose such talent, only because someone wants to take his spite out on Ed Hoak." He also chided national leaders by reminding them that "we speak of the democratic process in Boys' State . . . and other programs, but we sure don't practice it in our own organization."

Despite this, state legion leaders urged him to continue to build his candidacy, which he renewed in 1976. To spread his message, Hoak embarked on a national tour. He visited virtually every state. One visit took him to New Mexico, Texas, and Washington. From Las Cruces, New Mexico, on February 6, Hoak and Pennsylvania department commander John F. Titus accompanied national Commander Harry Wiles of Kansas on a tour of the White Sands Missile Range and White Sands National Monument. They were accompanied by the other 1976 candidate, William Rogers of Maine. That evening, the Pennsylvanians were feted by the New Mexico department. The following day, they departed for El Paso, Texas, where they stopped at Del Norte Post #58 and encountered Legionnaire Robert Kephart, formerly of Lock Haven, Pennsylvania. The group then traveled to Yakima, Washington, where members dined with local Legionnaires.

The next morning, Hoak presented himself to the department Executive Committee and gave his platform in a condensed form: "The American Legion, at all levels, must come down from the grandstands and get on the playing field, where the battle for people's minds is being fought." He said that all Legionnaires must become totally committed to new principles, including reform and regeneration. Hoak recommended that permanent sections within the national organization be created rather than continuing "a constant shifting of boundaries to satisfy [the] political considerations of vice commanders." Up until that point, the Legion had had five national vice commanders who represented the basic sections of the nation: southern, western, eastern, midwestern, and southwestern. These sections never changed, but various departments in border areas such as Nebraska, Utah, and Maryland could be shifted into another section upon a vote by the NEC. Hoak argued that some individuals lobbied for changes in order to set up a better opportunity for one of their department members to be appointed as national vice commander. In effect, the election of national vice commanders could be orchestrated in advance by those in power at the national headquarters in Indianapolis. He called for an end to bickering between the national headquarters and "dissenting departments." Finally, he asked that the Legion practice "true democracy" and demanded that it not be a rubber stamp for any government agency or officials. Hoak's campaign soon struck a chord with Legionnaires across the country. Kenneth Young, the adjutant from the Kansas department, supported Hoak, saying, "We are not bringing in a sufficient number of good, qualified Legionnaires." In an anonymous letter, a New York Legionnaire conceded that Hoak had some good ideas and that "they [the Legion leadership] should very well entertain new ideas and consider worthwhile projects wherever they come from."

Above all, Hoak and his fellow Pennsylvanians tried to revitalize the Legion's public image. This was crucial both for its future and the entitlements veterans had come to enjoy. Hoak wanted the independence bicentennial to set off a new Legion promotional campaign. In a speech at the West Virginia Americanism and Children & Youth Conference, Hoak urged veterans "to get involved in the big birthday party of our nation." He emphasized that "the name and prestige of the American Legion is formed at the local post level, not at the department or national headquarters, and that is how our neighbors get to know our organization, by what happens next door."

The campaign climaxed at the 58th national convention in Seattle. Three hundred Pennsylvania Legionnaires and Auxiliary members made an all-out effort on Hoak's behalf. The Pennsylvania department operated two hospitality rooms and about a dozen Pennsylvanians accompanied the candidate to the caucuses of other departments. When schedules conflicted, department leaders such as Bucky Campbell and alternate National Committeeman Steve Mikosky pitched Hoak's candidacy in his absence. Former department Commander Titus made the nominating speech.

Many pledges were made to support Hoak, but when the vote came, the national political machine, as some described it, had its ways of bringing opponents back in line. A straw vote taken the night before the election indicated that Hoak had at least eight hundred votes, in addition to Pennsylvania's unanimous vote. However, since some pro-Rogers departments came early in the alphabetical listing, many who had pledged votes to the Pennsylvania candidate "jumped on the bandwagon" when it became obvious that Rogers was ahead.

Hoak knew his candidacy was an uphill fight but considered it worthwhile "simply because of the issues that we raised." However, all the disappointment caused by Hoak's defeat was quickly eclipsed in a few months as the Pennsylvania Legion—and the nation at large—were faced with a disaster no one had been prepared for.

CHAPTER

6

FROM TRAGEDY TO TRIUMPH

*The Keystone Legion and
Legionnaires' Disease,
1976–77*

T hey walk with canes and have trouble breathing, these old
soldiers who are still in the clutches of the disease named
after them. Even now, when strangers see their American
Legion caps, some turn away or refuse to get into an elevator
with them. "It's funny now," recounted Russell Dugan, sixty-
eight, in an interview with the *Philadelphia Inquirer.* The
retired accountant from Wilkes-Barre, who was given the last
rites of his church when he was stricken by Legionnaires' disease on July 22, 1976, continued, "But it wasn't funny then."

Legionnaires who stayed at the Bellevue-Stratford Hotel in
Philadelphia during the summer of 1976 were struck down with
raging fevers and blood infections. Legionnaires' disease was a
mystery that in a short time generated immense fear, controversy, and public concern. The tragedy made it abundantly clear

that though Americans live in a medically advanced society, they can still be gripped by the terror of an unknown disease. "It is unsettling," said a senator who investigated the case, "to be living at a time when we have the know-how to put a man on the moon and yet can see a mysterious 'agent' sweep through a traditional American gathering, an annual convention, striking 182 people and causing twenty-nine deaths." By the end of 1977, there were more than 350 confirmed cases of Legionnaires' disease and seventy-five deaths in twenty-four states.

The 58th state convention was held at the Bellevue-Stratford Hotel while the 56th convention of the Auxiliary was being held at another hotel in the Philadelphia area. As usual, the convention attracted Legion delegates, Auxiliary members, family members, and Legionnaires who had no formal role. The prime activity—lobbying by office seekers—was conducted in hospitality suites maintained by the candidates. Most were open three or four days during the convention. Each district and many local posts also had hospitality rooms, scattered among several hotels.

It was the bicentennial year in what had been the premier Colonial city. Philadelphia, beset by a garbage strike and fiscal problems, badly needed the boost that the celebration would give to its economy. The Legion convention would do likewise. By the afternoon of the first day, Thursday, July 24, thousands of Legionnaires and spouses had gathered to attend sectional caucuses, lobby for their favorite sons for this or that office, vote on resolutions, and hear leading Legionnaires and guests. But this was to be more than a typical gathering: Long-time Adjutant Edward T. Hoak was to kick off his campaign for national commander. Many Pennsylvania Legionnaires believed Hoak's long record of accomplishment and service would aid in his quest for that position at the national convention in Seattle the next month.

The convention concluded without incident. Some recalled drinking more water than usual or the less-than-adequate conditions at the hotel, but nothing more extraordinary. Hoak said he became suspicious just days after the convention ended. He heard of an unusual number of ailing members, many of whom had the same symptoms: chills, fever, diarrhea, headaches, and respiratory difficulty. At first, news of several deaths did not alarm the adjutant: "We have a lot of elderly people, so it's not unusual to have a couple of deaths after a convention," he said. The victims, however, were not just the old and those already sick. More than a few of the deceased had been judged as vigorous at the convention.

On Saturday morning, July 31, 1976, Hoak journeyed to his hometown, Manor, 200 miles west of Harrisburg. He received a call from a friend who said he was coming down with some sort of flu but felt he could attend the installation ceremony for new officers of #472 in Manor that afternoon. As adjutant, Hoak was scheduled to speak. When he reached the Manor post, he was troubled to hear that a close friend along with six other Legionnaires were in the hospital. In addition, Frank Harvey, a Legionnaire and close friend, had just died in nearby McKeesport. Even so, the adjutant had no idea that throughout Pennsylvania, seventy-four people who had attended the convention were seriously ill.

On Sunday morning, August 1, Hoak returned to his residence in Camp Hill. When he got to Legion headquarters in Harrisburg in the evening, he opened a letter from Mrs. Elmer Hafer, informing him of her husband's illness, perhaps pneumonia. He wasn't responding to treatment. Soon, a flurry of phone conversations convinced Hoak of the gravity of the situation. He learned of the unexplained death of Charles Chamberlain, commander-elect of St. Thomas Post #612. Hoak then called Richard Snyder, a past state commander who lived in Williamsport, to inform him of Chamberlain's death and that of another friend, Elmer Hafer. Snyder told him that six people from Williamsport were hospitalized.

Hoak's first reaction was, "It's got to be something in western Pennsylvania. But I started to call other areas of the state and heard about other people who were sick. I'm convinced that if this had been any other group, nobody ever would have tied it together." Hoak then told the state commander, Joseph V. Adams of Cheltenham, of the tragic events. On Monday, August 2, Hoak learned of five more deaths and that about thirty more people were gravely ill. After conferring with the Pennsylvania Department of Health, a center was established to gather information on further illnesses across the state. Hoak worked until midnight for ten straight days, conferring with state and national health authorities.

The relationships among Legionnaires were thus vital to the investigation. "If it were a bunch of shoe salesmen who got together and fifteen or twenty of them died around the country, nobody would probably notice. But it's the nature of the organization—we're closer knit than most." Researchers and physicians from coast to coast came to admire the teamwork and sacrifice of the Pennsylvania Legion when faced with such a tragedy, something that could have caused lesser organizations to collapse.

Legionnaires' disease felled a number of hard-working and dedicated members. Some had served in the American Expeditionary Force during World War I or as GIs in the crusade against Hitler and Tojo. Abe Ruben, for example, survived combat in France in 1918 and the flu epidemic of 1919 before succumbing to Legionnaires' disease. He was a long-standing member of Cumberland Post #400 and the old Legion honor society, the Forty and Eight. Harold G. "Goose" Stump had been a sergeant in the 355th Engineering Company, which served in the Normandy invasion, northern France, the Rhineland, the Ardennes, and Central Europe. He earned an array of citations, including the European-African Middle Eastern Campaign Medal with five bronze stars. He was head steward of Post #71 in Milton. Julius Gaggiani was recipient of the first Man of the Year award by the Rotary Club in Republic and a member of Post #590 there. These victims were a cross-section of veterans who had served their country and community for more than fifty years.

A nearly perfect example of the quiet success exposed by the tragedy involved the Legion post in Williamstown. The authors of *Anatomy of an Epidemic,* an early study of the medical search for the cause of Legionnaires' disease, concentrated on the victims there. They were surprised to learn of the range of Legion activities. For nearly sixteen years, Richard "Dicko" Dolan and his brother Jimmy (one of the earliest victims) had belonged to Post #239. Neighbors and friends described it as a godsend in times of trouble. They still recalled how in 1972, when Hurricane Agnes roared through the area, Legionnaires had turned the post into a shelter for the hundreds of people driven from their homes by the flooding. Residents also remembered the petition campaign Dolan spearheaded that resulted in the bulldozing of burning mounds of coal dust that had blighted the outer reaches of the town for generations. The post run by Dicko Dolan also was famous for cutting red tape that often obstructed veterans in obtaining state and federal benefits.

Visiting journalists also learned of the important and multi-faceted role of a post in a small community. For more than half a century, it had been the center of social and civic life in Williamstown. The post sponsored "midget" and junior baseball leagues and Boy and Girl Scout troops, and bought uniforms, instruments, and flags for the high school band. Members joined with other veterans' organizations to form a Williamstown military band and donated a plot for the construction of a new armory. Post #239 also provided disabled veterans and their families with coal through the winter and food year-round. It organized transportation to and from the nearest VA facility. Dolan and other Legionnaires delivered medicines to any bedridden veteran who requested it. They bought the town a new fire truck with the most up-to-date equipment. Post #239 led the campaign to establish a new business in an abandoned mill, which paid off when a manufacturer employing more than 200 people took over the building.

Hoak, like his predecessors, served as the Legion's chief representative in the state. As such, his office served as a storm center for the emerging crisis. Hoak once described himself to a journalist as a sort of executive director in charge of dispensing information and advice to Pennsylvania's 890 posts. He had the confidence of members and the knowledge to gather information from all parts of the state. He contacted posts as to whether any members had fallen ill after returning from the convention. When he spoke to relatives of ailing veterans, he often told them to inform the physician in charge that perhaps others who had attended the convention from that area also were sick.

Eventually, Adams contacted the Legion's rehabilitation director, who alerted VA facilities across the state. Typhoid fever was the original diagnosis. When the death toll rose to three, Hoak contacted the Associated Press. "I didn't know how else to communicate with people all over the country," he said. People from California, Florida, and even Britain offered condolences, financial help, and theories as to the cause and treatment of the disease. Hoak quickly found himself on a first-name basis with researchers at the Centers for Disease Control in Atlanta. He continued to track dead and dying Legionnaires across the state. At the beginning of the "microbe hunt" his records were superior to those of the State Health Department. Survivors have consistently maintained that Hoak's quick and insistent action kept many of them alive.

Researchers later discovered that the disease is caused by bacteria that grow in the stagnant water that pools in air-conditioning systems, and this had happened at the Bellevue-Stratford. After comparing a number of cases, typical symptoms of Legionnaires' disease were found to be a rundown feeling, muscle aches, and a slight headache, followed by a rapidly rising fever, chills, and a dry cough. Stomach pains and cramps also developed in many victims. When the victim contacted a physician, often two to three days later, the fever exceeded 100 degrees and chest X-rays showed patchy pneumonia. One pathologist described the lungs of a deceased victim as simply "scary."

Before the reason was found, theories about the outbreak abounded, some of them sinister. George B. Chiavetta, a delegate and former post commander from the Harrisburg area, said he saw a man in a blue suit in the lobby of the hotel with what resembled a tobacco pouch containing something that could have poisoned the conventioneers. Victims and their families quickly blamed the Bellevue-Stratford. Even during the convention, the management received complaints about the rooms and other facilities. Delegate John Zweisdak insisted that bad housekeeping was responsible for spreading the bacteria. "I don't think any of the Legionnaires were happy about going there for the 1976 convention," he said. Three years later, he developed asthma and blamed his later bad health on Legionnaires' disease. To this day, however, not all Legionnaires are convinced of the explanation for the sickness. "I slept in the same room with Charles Mike," said Frank C. Andrukiewicz, a juvenile probation officer from Luzerne County. "I didn't get sick." But Mike, a retired letter carrier, later testified that the room's air-conditioning flow was blowing right on him, "and I did smell a bad odor while I was in bed."

Mike said he got a headache during the two-hour bus trip home to Wilkes-Barre. By the end of the trip, he was ready for the hospital, where he remained for nearly a month. He was packed in ice while fighting a 109-degree fever. Mike said, "I still go to the doctor. I'm always tired. . . . I'm always gasping for breath."

Russell Dugan also was mysteriously struck down. While he was in the hospital, another Legionnaire, Edwin Markiewicz of Nanticoke in Luzerne County, was working at a construction site nearby. He sneaked into Dugan's room each day to check on his condition. "They kept pouring alcohol on him," he said. "I didn't think he was going to make it."

"I was so close to death, I was in the tunnel," Dugan recollected. "You know how people who almost die say they go into a tunnel." There was such intense interest in the condition of the victims that doctors drew blood from him every fifteen minutes for several days. The samples were then flown to laboratories for instant analysis.

Most victims of the disease were initially unaware of the battle going on inside them between a deadly invader and their own defense system.

After the first flu-like symptoms, the infection would attack a patient's lungs. At this point, treatment with a powerful antibiotic, erythromycin, was often effective in driving back the invading organism. The recovery might last days, weeks, or months, but most victims survived.

Meanwhile, the initial investigations into the causes of the disease were raising more questions. At first, researchers suspected a virus; after a few weeks, they also looked at the possibility of some toxin. The investigation was primarily conducted at the U.S. Centers for Disease Control in Atlanta and by Dr. F. William Sunderman at the University of Connecticut Medical School. The CDC was pursuing the cause—officially, at least— without preconceptions, while Sunderman, one of the nation's leading experts on nickel poisoning, was searching intently for evidence that the illness was caused by nickel carbonyl, an industrial substance that could have induced the symptoms.

Another theory at the time was phosgene poisoning. This was put forth by Lorne F. Cook, a self-described consulting chemist from Wilmington, Delaware. He raised the possibility that the gas, a chemical weapon used by the Germans in World War I, had been created by a coolant leak and spread by the hotel's air-conditioning system. As a result, Legionnaires closest to the air-conditioning outlets would have been "gassed."

The media termed the affliction Legionnaires' disease because, whatever its origins, it seemed to be killing a disproportionate number of Pennsylvania Legionnaires. During the summer of 1976, the death toll reached twenty-nine. More than 150 veterans and their dependents were also hospitalized. One thing seemed certain: All seemed to have stayed at or visited the Bellevue-Stratford Hotel from July 21–24.

The hotel itself was a casualty of the disease, as Hoak noted in his testimony before the House investigating committee on November 24, 1976. In fact, the impact was almost immediate. Conventions and other events scheduled to take place at the Bellevue were abruptly canceled and sometimes moved out of town. An investigation by *Philadelphia Magazine* discovered that Miami's tourist bureau had persuaded no fewer than seven major groups to switch from Philadelphia. Despite a massive attempt to counter the impact of the disease outbreak, the hotel's occupancy rate plunged from eighty-five percent before July 21 to 10 to 20 percent by the autumn of 1976. Eventually, the Bellevue-Stratford was sold to a local developer who, with a national chain, almost totally revamped the structure and character of the hotel.

Time has healed many of the physical and emotional harms wrought by Legionnaires' disease, but bad memories remain. Years later, Hoak good-naturedly recalled the initial feeling of repulsion felt by many people toward Legionnaires as a group. This was first noticed by the Pennsylvania delegation at the national convention in Seattle. In a lengthy interview with the *Cincinnati Inquirer* ten years after the outbreak, Hoak told of the waitress who asked whether he had heard about the "bizarre disease" that had killed the conventioneers. He told the waitress that he had been at the center of the tragedy. After he ate, she broke all the dishes he had used and threw them in the trash.

What angered Hoak and other Legionnaires were the difficulties that many patients had in paying their medical bills. Hoak knew that few of the sick Legionnaires could meet the costs of a "battery of unexpected tests and intensive care nursing." Some were under pressure to pay their bills immediately or face cutoff of treatment. Hoak was infuriated to learn of one hospital administrator who was "closing in on one patient, even threatening to take his house." The adjutant attempted to stop such harassment and organized fund-raising efforts to aid veterans and their families in financial need because of Legionnaires' disease.

In a memorial at Legion headquarters in Harrisburg, there is a testament to the thirty-eight men and women who died . Since the Philadelphia convention, Hoak said he and fellow veterans have learned a few things. "It made us all a lot more concerned about each other," he stated. "We now look out for each other a little more. We keep up with each other a little more. We're closer." As the controversy passed, interest in the disease among the public—and Legionnaires—declined. The survivors started the Legionnaires' Disease Club and met once in Pittsburgh. They all received cards certifying that they had been victims. Since they could not think of anything else to do, there have been no more scheduled meetings.

The memorial in Harrisburg was created as a permanent reminder of the Legion's role in identifying the disease. In 1977, national headquarters honored Hoak with a plaque and said his efforts probably spared hundreds more from a disease that, if diagnosed early, is relatively easy to treat. Earlier, Hoak had been awarded the Pennsylvania Legion's Distinguished Service Medal for the same reason. For a time, there were hard feelings within the Legion among members who did not want to be identified with the disease. Hoak, who did so much to further the investigation, opposed their efforts to disassociate the Legion from the disease. "I think it's a tribute to the people who died because they alerted the country to a deadly disease," he said. Changing the name "would be a disservice to those who suffered and brought this to the attention of the medical profession and the general public." Survivors of the affliction concurred. "I told them to leave it the way it was," Russell Dugan said. "After all, we're the ones who went through it."

STANDING GUARD

*The Keystone Legion
and the Challenges
of the Present*

fter 1976, the Keystone Legion was faced with new challenges and old problems. The debate over whether to
admit Vietnam veterans was settled, but the question
remained of how best to encourage them to join. Moreover, the
power of the American Legion and all veterans' organizations
was challenged by the changing political climate. The next fifteen years saw the officers and rank and file of the Pennsylvania
American Legion weather the storm and come out intact.

The Legion celebrated the bicentennial in word and deed. In
preparation for the festivities, at its April 1975 meeting in
Williamsport, the department Executive Committee established
the Pennsylvania American Legion Bicentennial Project. Officials commissioned a hand-made reproduction of a Durham
boat, the type that took George Washington and his troops

across the Delaware, at a cost of $10,000. Three thousand of this was raised by the department Auxiliary. Many more bicentennial projects were organized or supported by Legionnaires across the state.

The year 1976 was not simply a national celebration of the bicentennial. Also because of Legionnaires' disease, business-as-usual attitudes disappeared. After the crisis, it was time to pick up the pieces and resume life. The Keystone Legion also showed signs of change. 1977 membership saw a decrease of 6,000 from the 1976 total of 262,000. Hoak said later, "The decrease can be at least partially attributed to the Legionnaires' disease, which affected many of our key personnel and greatly reduced the time they could give to the Legion when a new membership year was just beginning." He also conceded that the aftermath of the Vietnam War was hurting recruitment, following seventeen years of record membership. Even so, Pennsylvania eventually placed fourth in membership among the fifty-eight departments.

To compensate, in part, the Executive Committee in May 1977 recommended a seventy-five-cent dues increase for 1978. The department's problems in the late Seventies were part of the larger economic malaise felt by the United States. The increase in energy costs and the pressure for staff salary increases caused by general inflation caught the department in a bind: raise dues or cut services. Hoak explained that even if spending were unchanged, the department would show a deficit of $62,000. The state department retained only $1.70 from each Legionnaire's dues of $3.50, since five cents was marked for the Scotland School and the rest went to national headquarters.

The budget of 1977–78 could have been balanced by cuts, but at the cost of programs, activities, and services vital to the Legion. Hoak pointed out that this could reduce the number of service officers at a time when more and more World War II veterans and their dependents needed help. "The fact that membership is slipping," he added, "means that we should be putting more emphasis on it, rather than cutting back."

The adjutant also pointed out that the national dues average was $3.85, with only one department charging less than Pennsylvania and others as much as $7.85. Also, eleven states subsidized their departments' rehabilitation programs, in one case contributing half a million dollars to nursing homes, home care, and disability programs for veterans. Pennsylvania's program ran entirely on state Legion contributions. Members at the 59th department convention approved the increase, as they had whenever state headquarters requested it. Throughout the department's history, per capita dues remained consistently lower than the national average.

The economic malaise in the late 1970s was sometimes seen in the mood of veterans and their relationship to the Legion. Within the state, the nuclear accident at Three Mile Island near Harrisburg in March 1979 may have contributed to this unease. Even though the Keystone Legion was ready (Middletown's Post #594 served as the media center during the incident), it was felt that little could be done to help events. Many outside observers felt that the Legion was out of touch with the nation and the latest generation of veterans. One TV commentator in Philadelphia called the Legion a fossil and denied that it had a future. The feeling touched Legionnaires as well. In November 1977, a newspaper in Delaware County interviewed Jules Falcone of Radnor, the 8th District commander.

"There were times," he said, "when veterans were literally clamoring to join the American Legion. . . . Those times came on the heels of this nation's involvement in two major world wars. . . . Veterans could readily identify with veterans' organizations." But now, he was "the first to admit veterans, especially Vietnam vets, haven't been beating down the doors" of his post home, Bateman-Gallagher Post #668 of Wayne, or any of the other fifty-two American Legion posts in Delaware and Chester counties." At the same time, he noted that "an increasing number of Vietnam era veterans are turning to the Legion, not so much for traditional reasons—the bonuses and the benefits—but to be part of a viable, community service-oriented veterans' organization." Eventually, as many of their older comrades had discovered, Vietnam veterans found the Legion to be a forum for veterans' needs and issues.

Falcone's post was among the first to consciously and successfully recruit Vietnam veterans. One who joined the Bateman-Gallagher post was Falcone's son, Flavio. He discovered Legion membership was not only "a ticket to community social contacts" but a "vehicle for stimulating challenges and remarkable personal rewards." He was one of the fifty or so Vietnam veterans who made up a fifth of the post's membership. They were not just "card carriers" but extremely active; several were involved in Legion baseball and service work with the disabled in nearby hospitals. "It's taken us years to get a good input from Korea vets and the same holds true for Vietnam vets," Jules Falcone said in the interview.

The Falcones were the first in their post to help organize unemployment workshops for Vietnam veterans. A local newspaper said these were well attended and greatly helped spread the word about the Legion. More significantly, they often provided the first opportunity for Vietnam veterans to gather and discuss matters of common interest. Rocky Bleier, a Vietnam veteran, a former Pittsburgh Steeler, and a Legionnaire, was at such a meeting in McKeesport and went out of his way to encourage fellow veterans to find out what the Legion had to offer. Once these contacts were established, it became easier for veterans to take the first step and join their local post. A VA official later referred to the department's unemployment workshops as the best thing ever for showing Vietnam veterans they were not alone and their problems were surmountable.

When Flavio joined, he sought to bring in other Vietnam era veterans whom he met at school. He recruited several fraternity brothers from nearby Villanova University. By the end of the decade, half of Bateman-Gallagher's elected officers were college graduates. Flavio rose to vice chairman for youth and children's activities in the Pennsylvania department.

The elder Falcone noted the generational differences between his contemporaries and those of his son. These younger veterans "were given more to reflect than reminisce, to sort out the personal, social, and political ramifications of an unpopular war." Many resumed education and careers interrupted by military service. "Only now," Jules Falcone explained, "are some of these men finding time for social contacts and community activities." In short, as men of the Vietnam generation grew older, they became concerned and involved in the issues of their community, state, and nation.

Certainly, the Legion was involved in plenty of issues. After 1976, the Pennsylvania department joined the campaign to oppose the Carter administration's proposal to return the Panama Canal to Panama by the year 2000. The Americanism chairman from the 27th District wrote Senator John Heinz that he was "thoroughly disenchanted with your vote on the issue [of the treaty] on March 16." Within the state, opinion was divided. Many of its leading newspapers sided with the Carter administration. The *Pittsburgh Post-Gazette* noted that "Pennsylvania's delegation in the House of Representatives turned in a worse [from the paper's point of view] performance than the House as a whole, voting 13–11 *against* the administration's impending legislation." Senator Heinz voted for the treaty and Senator Richard Schweiker voted against it.

Daniel Drew, a longtime national committeeman and the department's Americanism chairman, led the Legion drive against the Panama Canal treaty. The rank and file was vocal in its criticism of the president's proposed policy. James W. Slasser, a member of Post #161 in Westford, wrote: "Why talk to him [Panamanian General Omar Torrijos], since he is a dictator? . . . How or why should we deal with him at all? By your submission to the threats of a tinhorn dictator," the Legionnaire continued, "you have made almost certain that Communist troops will be in Panama and the canal will be nationalized within a few years." Several Legion posts in the Pittsburgh area suggested that the United States should remove Torrijos by force. Ironically, more than a decade later, American servicemen removed his successor, Manuel Antonio Noriega, in this fashion.

The Keystone Legion used a number of publications, including the *Legion-gram,* to mobilize opposition to the bill. Department Commander Eugene C. Eichelberger urged members to persuade Heinz to reverse his position on the treaty. Within a week in late 1977, more than 50,000 postcards were sent to the state's two senators from people who identified themselves as Legionnaires or friends of the Legion. Through Legion pressure, the treaty came to a second vote and was passed with modifications. Even this didn't please some Legionnaires. Post #544 of Minersville lowered its flag to half-staff as a symbolic protest.

Of immediate concern to Vietnam veterans was that many of them had been exposed to the defoliant Agent Orange. Hoak wrote to the Pennsylvania congressional delegation: "We in the Legion strongly feel that existing legislation and regulations do not provide adequate due process for the veterans exposed to such toxic substances in Vietnam." He testified before a House subcommittee on the controversy. He noted how the Pennsylvania Department of Health had assisted during the Legionnaires' disease crisis and could "do likewise . . . with the Vietnam veterans and their families who are suffering from 'Agent Orange.'" Hoak affirmed the Legion's support for House Bill 1763 and urged research on other possible chemical weapons used in Southeast Asia.

The Keystone Legion supported federal legislation to research Agent Orange-related illness and treat the effects. The bill was introduced by two friends and supporters of the Legion, George E. Saurman of Montgomery County and Paul I. Clymer of Bucks County. The bill sought a two-year study on Agent Orange illnesses and a maximum $5,000 benefit per affected veteran. In addition, the Keystone Legion provided an Agent Orange hot line manned by Legionnaires, health care professionals, and Vietnam veterans.

The Keystone Legion became sensitive, in time, to the image of the Vietnam veteran. One incident brought the Legion to the attention of many Vietnam veterans in Pennsylvania. On Veterans' Day, November 11, 1981, the Public Broadcasting Service planned to show a two-hour film, "Frank: A Vietnam Veteran," the story of a veteran who had had bouts with alcoholism and drug abuse, divorce, unemployment, and occasional mental breakdowns. While PBS stated that "Frank" was not intended to represent the "typical" Vietnam veteran, many vets feared that the public would think he did.

The *Times* of Norristown stated, "The American Legion says the program portrays veterans as social and moral deviants and they [local veterans] say it would be a travesty if the show was aired." Harrisburg's *Patriot News* reported that the Pennsylvania War Veterans' Council had officially objected to the showing of the film. One Vietnam veteran and Legionnaire feared that the stereotype of the Vietnam veteran would be reinforced. The department's commander, Victor Raia of Altoona, called the documentary a gross disservice to the Vietnam veteran that would simply "reinforce certain prejudices. . . . If the film is a salute to veterans, we don't need it."

The Keystone Legion also was mindful of the image of the Vietnam veteran in the popular film industry. An assembly of Legionnaires, including Activities Director Stanley Reinhard,

Hoak, and Assistant Adjutant Harvey Coleman, blasted Oliver Stone's movie "Platoon," saying it offered unfair and speculative images of American actions in Vietnam. Instead, the Legion recommended "Hanoi Hilton," a film that it said presented a far more realistic picture of the enemy and the fate of American prisoners of war. The fate of the MIAs/POWs still in Southeast Asia became a lively topic among Legion members. In order to keep this issue alive, the Keystone Legion organized "living memorials" for POWs still thought to be in captivity. In January 1985, a POW-MIA candlelight service was held on the capitol steps in Harrisburg.

As in previous decades, the issue of veterans' care, particularly for the elderly, was a political football. State legislators often opposed these programs because of cost and portrayed themselves as guardians of the taxpayer. One such case arose in the spring of 1976, when various politicians opposed the conversion of Valley Forge General Hospital into a nursing home for veterans. Hoak said, "I think that the state is neglecting its responsibility to more than a million and a half veterans. . . . The very fact that there are only 175 beds for veterans in the commonwealth indicates how desperate it is." The Keystone Legion compared Pennsylvania's number of beds for incapacitated veterans to those of other states: California, 1,350; Oklahoma, 1,134; Illinois, 959; Ohio, 816; and Wisconsin, 726. As a result of Legion pressure, the hospital remained open.

Persistence could pay off. Pennsylvania Legionnaires helped carry a resolution at the 60th national convention in New Orleans in the fall of 1978 that asked Congress to provide World War I veterans with a guaranteed pension. For eighteen years, the Keystone Legion had sought an automatic pension for veterans of the Great War. A year earlier, at the convention in Denver, a similar resolution had been defeated by a narrow margin.

As usual, the successful resolution was the result of compromise and maneuvering. Ray Breen of the Illinois department helped organize the support as he had done in previous years. Speakers from Texas, Ohio, and New Jersey endorsed it, as did Hoak. Dr. Almo J. Sebastianelli, the department's national committeeman, lobbied for the resolution at caucuses and informal meetings. Many World War I veterans were gratified but said that they had waited a long time for this measure. A veteran from

Pottsville wrote Legion headquarters that he was renewing a long-lapsed membership at his local post because of the passage of this measure by the Legion and later by Congress. By the late 1980s, veterans of World War I were only ineligible for the GI Bill's education benefits and home loan guarantee program. Certainly, not all of these veterans were happy with pension benefits, but giant strides were made in these years to achieve equity with the later generations of veterans.

The Keystone Legion also was alarmed by the emerging crisis of care in VA facilities and rest homes. Of particular concern was the Erie Soldiers and Sailors Home in western Pennsylvania. Steve Mikosky, department commander for 1977–78, said the building was in deplorable condition. He and the department conceded that the state, which was responsible for the home, had recently improved conditions somewhat, but more was required. Mikosky and Hoak followed up a visit to the Erie home with one to the state prison in Greenburg, where they said living conditions were much better. Further improvements were made, but the Keystone Legion kept an eye on conditions in Erie.

In April 1985, the Keystone Legion opposed President Reagan's controversial decision to lay a wreath at the German military cemetery at Bitburg. The department's commander, L.G. Smith, noted that the cemetery contained the graves of SS officers who may have overseen the killing of U.S. prisoners of war during the Battle of the Bulge. At the same time, the Pennsylvania Legion stayed out of matters that were not of immediate interest to veterans. Thomas Makar, commander of Nuremberg Post #669, would not permit an anti-abortion group to hold a mock trial of the Supreme Court in the post home in the autumn of 1985. The post had been chosen by a Chicago-based anti-abortion organization because it was named after the site of the World War II war crimes trials.

As in the previous decade, the Keystone Legion played a role in the national organization. In 1980, Tom Cammarota, past department commander and national committeeman, announced he was running for national commander in 1982. "PA Legion maverick faces uphill election battle," declared a headline in the *Philadelphia Inquirer*. That was the reaction of many, inside and outside of the Legion. Cammarota, a fifty-seven-year-old former Marine, criticized the national organization for setting up one generally unopposed candidate each year. "It's at least forty years since we've had a national commander from Pennsylvania," he said, and indicated that change was necessary in certain Legion policy. "It is becoming more of a social program rather [than] a veterans' operation," he asserted.

As a Legionnaire, Cammarota had certainly worked hard for veterans' causes. In 1969, he helped to organize the controversial campaign to have Philadelphia name its new sports complex Veterans Stadium. Before it became department policy, Cammarota welcomed Vietnam veterans to his Germantown post. In 1970, he strongly disapproved on behalf of the Pennsylvania Legion of the reinstatement of Muhammad Ali by the nation's boxing promoters. In 1973, he told a Philadelphia audience that those who evaded the draft during Vietnam "should be tried as deserters." Cammarota contended that the Legion should be in the limelight and "I would be the national commander who could and would put it there."

Of particular significance to Cammarota were the real and projected cuts in veterans' benefits in the state and nation. "Vets are really suffering," he maintained. "We should be setting up programs to get more jobs for our veterans." In several interviews, Cammarota cited the Erie home as an example of what veterans had to contend with. He wanted veterans to be able to just walk into a clinic rather than travel to a distant VA hospital. The VA system could also be reinvigorated, in Cammarota's opinion, by employing former military medical personnel. The Cammarota campaign used catchy bumper stickers and slogans to illustrate these themes. A campaign button read, "To eliminate the waste, get a plumber." A bumper sticker declared that Cammarota was "A man for all reasons." In his campaign material, Cammarota said veterans who had been exposed to Agent Orange needed special help and had been getting the runaround from the VA.

A lack of funds restricted Cammarota's campaigning to the East. Hoak, the state adjutant who had run for national office in 1976, explained the problems of an "outsider" during an interview with the *Philadelphia Inquirer.* "I spent over $36,000, I traveled all over the country, all to no avail," he said. Cammarota was opposed by Al Keller of Illinois, who had been unofficially endorsed by the Legion's national leadership. Hoak stated that "no one in my lifetime, and I've been here since 1961," had ever successfully bucked the system. Hoak's word proved to be prophetic; Cammarota withdrew shortly before the Chicago convention began.

In September 1984, Hoak withdrew his name from the list of potential candidates for national commander. He recalled in an interview with the Harrisburg *Patriot News* that he made his decision when "he learned that Jimmy Dean was invited to open a hospitality room" by the Legion's national leadership. Dean was considered a reliable candidate and his stands on certain issues were sympathetic to those of the Keystone Legion. Hoak's decision was partly based upon his age (sixty), but he continued to work for the reforms that had characterized his earlier campaign. Pennsylvania sought at the 1985 national convention to change the way national vice commanders were chosen, to no avail. Some considered it yet another snub of Pennsylvania.

The Pennsylvania Legion took on major issues in the early 1980s. In late 1981, John Zweisdak, past department commander and then chairman of the Veterans Affairs and Rehabilitation Committee, urged the state Executive Committee to file a class-action suit against the Veterans Administration on behalf of the 50,000 veterans suffering from Agent Orange illnesses. He also urged that the national organization support President Reagan's 1981 budget, which would restore $600 million of the $800 million to be cut from the VA budget. The committee also petitioned the Army to reinstate the audible saying of prayers at ceremonies at the Tomb of the Unknown Soldier in Arlington National Cemetery and to "make certain that no organization be allowed to conduct a ceremony for political purposes" there. The committee also urged the Legion's Children and Youth Commission to study child abuse.

The worst fears of Legionnaires were realized in Congress's "deficit fever" in 1985 and its decision to cut spending on veterans. Medical care was to be restricted to those with strictly service-connected disabilities, former prisoners of war, pensioners, and sick veterans "with demonstrated needs." The proposed cuts were the result of studies conducted by the Grace Commission as well as those of the Reagan administration's Office of Management and Budget.

The department leadership had reason to be concerned. Pennsylvania in the mid-Eighties was the home of more than 1,500,000 veterans, 276,000 of whom were more than sixty-five years old. This group would almost double in size by the year 2000. Without the VA medical system, they would have to be cared for by Pennsylvania's public hospitals, which already were under severe strain. The Keystone Legion strictly opposed restricting veterans' benefits according to need. This stand awakened many Legionnaires as to how times had changed. Now there were hundreds of special interests fighting for a share of the federal budget.

The Keystone Legion followed the lead of the national organization in setting up conferences to discuss strategy. This was aided immeasurably by Pennsylvania Senator Arlen Specter, who fought to preserve military installations such as the Philadelphia Navy Yard. He led Pennsylvania Legionnaires in Washington at strategy sessions throughout the 1980s. The ranking Republican on the Senate Veterans Affairs Committee, Specter first learned of the Legion through his father, who helped support his family on a $23-a-month disability check after World War I. This sensitized him to the issues involved in the long budget battles. Specter worked tirelessly for veterans in Pennsylvania and often contacted Legion officers on floor votes that pertained to veterans.

The 1986 department convention was dominated by the deficit-reduction legislation, called the Gramm-Rudman bill after two of its sponsors. The 68th convention went on record as opposing the means test to be applied to veteran hospital care. Judge Advocate Robert W. Valimont of Doylestown argued that "the imposition of a means test under the guise of economy" would mean the end of the VA system. Such benefits were not "gratuities or charitable gifts . . . and should not be limited to those who are impoverished." The most controversial resolution to come before the convention was a condemnation of apartheid in South Africa. The Resolutions Committee recommended its rejection, but the delegates approved it anyway. This was despite a warning by the keynote speaker, former Secretary of State Alexander Haig.

More than 1,000 veterans demonstrated at ten VA medical centers in Pennsylvania on Saturday, May 26, 1990. Fred Wagner, department commander in 1989–90, said, "These demonstrations will show to the U.S. Congress and the American people our dissatisfaction with the cuts of veterans' benefits took opposition to placing veterans in the classifications of A, B, and C to qualify for medical treatment. B and C veterans are already being denied medical care. . . . When we entered the military service, there were no A, B, or C categories." Veterans demanded the same dignity as other citizens and organized for that purpose.

The Keystone Legion continued to fight for Americanism, as its constitution required. The Legion joined more than a dozen other veterans' groups in the state in criticizing Senate candidate Bob Edgar for accepting money from a California-based fund-raising group, the Hollywood Political Action Committee, which included Jane Fonda. The Pennsylvania department also voted to "boycott Fonda's exercise books and spas." Legionnaires picketed her appearance at the Penn Harris Motor Inn near Harrisburg in 1982 when she spoke against nuclear power. In 1989, the department convention unanimously rejected her apology to veterans for her activities during the Vietnam era.

Pennsylvania, like most of the nation, was hurt by the recessions and inflation of the 1970s and 1980s. The department could not help but come to the aid of Pennsylvanians, veterans and non-veterans. In an unprecedented move in October 1987, department Commander Ronald F. Conley of Scott Township directly asked all Americans, not just veterans, to "honor Pearl Harbor" by permanently boycotting foreign-made products. Conley's public announcement came partly as a result of his reading about a $10 million contract awarded to Japan's Toshiba company despite several bids by American corporations. "If American companies can't supply our defense forces in peacetime," Conley argued, "who would do it in wartime? Would we depend on a questionable source for critical electronics in a national emergency?" Conley, a forty-three-year-old steamfitter, knew only too well the effects of foreign competition. He stated that his "own Pittsburgh home area is now termed a part of the Rust Belt because of cheap steel imports, including those from Japan."

The Pennsylvania Legion also pushed for a major legislative package to aid veterans across the country. The Pennsylvania department had long sought money to retrain middle-aged and recently unemployed veterans. Pennsylvania Legionnaires often appeared in Washington in the 1980s to promote legislation ranging from better comprehensive aid to tighter controls on immigration. Legion spokesmen also expressed concern "for the worker veteran in his fifties who has spent twenty to thirty years with a firm but loses his job through technology and other changes in industry."

The Keystone Legion in the late 1980s also supported state issuance of mortgage revenue bonds for home loans to veterans, the establishment of a state department of veterans affairs, preservation of the state veterans preference in Civil Service exams for state and municipal employment, and establishment of a new state veterans home in Pennhurst. It also urged a fund for the perpetual care of state veterans' homes and opposed any change in the state school code that would remove compulsory teaching of American history. The Legion also opposed the closing of military installations in the state.

The department Executive Committee met on January 23–24, 1988, to discuss international and local issues. It heard several speakers, including one from the rebels fighting the Sandinista government in Nicaragua. The committee urged the state Legislature to allow "small games of chance" to help local posts compete for charity business. It asked Congress to extend the wartime dates for Vietnam veterans from December 21, 1961, to May 7, 1975, so that they could be eligible for VA benefits, especially non-service disability pensions.

Diversity in leadership as well as membership was realized in the 1980s. In 1983, at the department convention in Pittsburgh, F. Rodney Loper of West Chester's Nathan Holmes Post #362 became the first African-American to be elected department commander. In 1988, another African-American, Horace V. Pippin of West Chester, was given posthumous recognition as a Legionnaire and artist. Women also were often post officers and commanders by this time. The Helen Fairchild nurses post in the Philadelphia area had been led by women for decades. In March 1989, the Mountaintop Post #781 elected its first female commander, Scottie Ann Kosielnik.

The Keystone Legion opposed the awarding of $20,000 to each Japanese-American interned during World War II. This was viewed as excessive in light of the $1-a-day compensation allowed for American POWs during the war. Hoak explained, "Just the matter of the amount involved . . . over $1 billion . . . we feel with the country's tight budget . . . should make anyone think twice. The American Legion is particularly concerned that as veterans benefits are being cut . . . we are considering a billion-dollar grant that we believe is not fully satisfied."

In May 1989, the department Executive Committee urged Congress to change the cost of repossessed housing from 40 percent of the market price to $1. This would aid the homeless—veterans and non-veterans. Earlier in the year, the committee had urged each district commander to appoint a panel on homeless veterans. On defense policy, the department asked legislators to reject any proposal or agreement on American-Japanese co-production of the FSX fighter plane. It urged Congress to take another look at the Medicare "catastrophic coverage" law and exclude from taxation those who have such coverage under other programs as well as "extend the tax to taxpaying citizens of all ages." The Pennsylvania department also worked incessantly to keep alive local posts. It worked with the Pennsylvania War Veterans Committee to lobby successfully for legalization of gambling devices such as video poker machines in veterans' clubs. These could attract a steady flow of customers.

The 1989 national convention saw a new push by the Keystone Legion to shape policy. A number of its resolutions were approved. One urged Congress to prohibit the sale of American goods to Communist countries; another wanted to increase benefits for "notch babies" in the Social Security system. More significantly, positions on eligibility of all veterans for membership softened, according to one convention delegate, for the first time in years. A quiet push for Dominic DiFrancesco for national commander also began.

Throughout the Eighties, homelessness gained increasing attention. More than half of these individuals, according to several studies, were veterans. Elizabeth Hanford Dole, a cabinet secretary, said at the 71st national convention, "These . . . veterans are still on the bottom of the ladder and have not been able to fully participate in the economic recovery."

The Keystone Legion supported homeless veterans in deeds as well as words. In late 1988, Ron Conley and other department officers began an innovative program for aiding homeless and drug-dependent veterans. The idea developed in part from a suggestion by a local Legionnaire and VA caseworker, Vinnie Malec, that an abandoned four-unit home in the Pittsburgh area be purchased for that purpose. Conley, the department commander, raised more than $20,000 for the purchase of the home under the Property Rehabilitation Act of 1987. It allowed a non-profit organization like the Pennsylvania Legion to buy repossessed property at a discount if it were to be used to assist homeless veterans. No federal funds were used to purchase or rehabilitate the housing.

"Here we have a place to call our own and a chance to start over," a homeless Vietnam veteran, Stanley D., said. "Everyone who lies here has hit rock bottom, so we understand and help each other." Veterans living in the home had to provide "sweat equity" in helping to repair and maintain their units. Rent was $50 a month and each had to pay his own utilities. In exchange for lower rent, one veteran was designated house leader. He or she had to collect rent, make utility payments, and ensure that maintenance was performed. "We apply the principles that we learned in the service," one resident mentioned in a TV interview. "Everyone pitches in and no one shirks his duty." In time, these veterans formed a carpet-cleaning business to support the home and themselves. This pilot program was imitated by other Legion departments and voluntary organizations across the country. It was lauded in the press, including the *New York Times,* as an example of local initiative and policy innovation.

The program was accepted by the delegates at the 70th annual convention of the Pennsylvania department, held in Valley Forge. Earlier, the DEC had approved $25,000 for the pilot program in Allegheny County. The proposal by Ron Conley of Pittsburgh invoked considerable debate, largely because of a concern that the department would be held liable for actions of individual residents or in financial failures. In fact, the motion was originally tabled and referred to the Legion's Judge Advocate, Doylestown's Robert Valimont, for further study. Valimont, however, took the floor and assured the committee that Legion liability could be avoided if a separate corporation were formed to operate the project.

The aid and compassion of the Keystone Legion had been extended to other unfortunates in the past. The Scotland School for Veterans' Children has long been a cherished Legion charity. It was founded in 1895 to educate the children of military personnel and veterans. From its early years, the Keystone Legion has supported the school with time and money, and at commencements and holidays, Legion officers partake in its proceedings and festivities. Members of the department's Auxiliary have annually presented class rings and gifts to "adopted" students, and the school's amphitheater was largely funded by Legion efforts. Several other projects and programs at the Scotland School owe their success to the Keystone Legion.

At the end of 1989, the Pennsylvania department stood at 270,353 members. Each section of the state topped its 1989 membership goal, leading Hoak to say, "It was apparent that more and more veterans of our most recent wars, Korea and Vietnam, are recognizing the need to belong to a veterans' organization." Pennsylvania had two of the fifty largest posts in the nation: Smedley D. Butler Post #701 in McKeesport, 2,132 members (twenty-second in the country), and Lancaster Post #34, 2,002 (thirty-second).

On August 29, 1990, delegates at the 72nd national convention asked Congress to amend the Legion's charter to allow membership to veterans of the actions in Grenada (1983) and Panama (1989). The last revision had been in 1979, when Vietnam veterans were allowed to join. Thus, 1990 witnessed the quiet triumph of the Keystone Legion's longtime goals. In 1946, its membership had peaked at about 304,000. This had dwindled to 238,000 by 1965, so a membership of 270,000 and above in the early Nineties is no small accomplishment. Since 1945, Pennsylvania has been the largest department and has about 10 percent of the national membership of 2,800,000. This is significant because the state has only 5.6 percent of the nation's veterans and its veteran population is exceeded by those of California (2,800,000), New York (1,800,000), and Texas (1,800,000).

The Nineties have reminded civilians and veterans alike of the fragility of peace. The United States formed the backbone of the

United Nations-endorsed coalition created to force Iraqi with-drawal from Kuwait after it invaded the Persian Gulf kingdom in August 1990. The Pennsylvania Legion organized rallies in sup-port of Operation Desert Storm in Philadelphia, Altoona, Harris-burg, Johnstown, Pendel, Scranton, Somerset, and Wilkes-Barre. It organized a hot-line network to aid families of troops. Com-mander Ray Lenz and other department officers attended memo-rial services for the twenty-nine Pennsylvanians who died during the conflict. On Flag Day 1991, department headquarters in Har-risburg dedicated a new memorial to the fallen.

For many in the Keystone Legion, Hobart Hopkins, a World War I veteran who had attended the Paris Caucus, was a living symbol of the Legion. A contemporary of Eric Fisher Wood and Franklin D'Olier, Hopkins had at one time toured the state to help organize the department. At that moment, 350,000 veter-ans had just been released from service. Seventy years later, there were a few thousand left. Until his death in a nursing home in 1991, Hopkins had been a member of the same Legion post for seven decades. "Once," Hopkins recalled in 1988, "I thought we'd become like the Grand Army of the Republic. . . . Instead, with every few generations or so, the Legion becomes alive again, like the Tree of Liberty the Founding Fathers talked about." Most of the Pennsylvanians who joined the Legion with Hopkins came from farms and small towns. Those who followed him often were raised in different circumstances, but all shared a common vision and purpose written in the Legion's preamble in 1919: "For God and Country, we associate ourselves together."

In 1992, the department and the state mourned the passing of Ed Hoak, who served for twenty-eight years as state adjutant. During his tenure, great changes took place. He supervised the construction of a new department headquarters valued at $500,000 at the time it was built. He founded the Pennsylvania American Legion Leadership School (Legion College) and helped to sponsor everything from senior veterans' information semi-nars to holiday visitations to VA medical centers. In his last year as adjutant, Hoak worked with many others toward a constitu-tional amendment to prohibit flag burning. He helped organize and edit the *Pennsylvania Keystone News,* called one of the best veterans' publications in the country. During his time, the Keystone Legion was brought into the modern age with a computer system containing information on members.

Perhaps the most fitting monument to Hoak is on the lawn in front of department headquarters. Four statues have been erected: a doughboy, a sailor from World War II, a Korean War Air Force pilot, and a Vietnam War Marine. There also is Memorial Wall to honor Pennsylvanians killed during undeclared military conflicts, Panama and the Persian Gulf being the most recent. The Keystone Legion has for more than seven decades existed to represent the people in uniform memorialized in these statues. As the twentieth century draws to a close, it will continue to do so with dignity and honor.

CHAPTER

8

ENDURING AMERICANISM

*The Keystone Legion and
Youth Activities from
1925 to the Present*

O ne of the most enduring challenges of the nation—its
youth—was from the start the most significant of concerns for the American Legion. Over the years, the Pennsylvania department combined patriotic education with
exercise and entertainment. Junior baseball, Boys' State, and
the Sons of the Legion have endeavored to train the body and
mind of America's youth. For the first generation of the American Legion, which had seen the value of teamwork on the fields
of France, organized sports taught the values of sacrifice for a
common purpose. Stanley Reinhard, the department commander in 1993 and longtime activities director, first encountered
the Legion in his hometown of Copley through the Junior baseball team. "Without Legion baseball," Reinhard recalled, "I

would not have been introduced to the principles of fair play and teamwork" that were part of both military and adult life.

The Legion sought to embody and promote "100 percent Americanism" from the start. The first Legion generation developed an extensive youth program. The early oratorical contests, essay contests, and flag education were usually conducted at schools. In the Legion's first five years, national conventions affirmed citizenship instruction in schools and the importance of "patriotic exercises," and recommended that Legion posts cooperate with school authorities "to instill the ideals of patriotism in the hearts of future generations."

From its early years to the present, youth baseball has been a prominent part of the American Legion. Historians have noted how these activities served as gateways to Legion membership. Legion baseball was fueled by a desire to improve the physical fitness of future generations and a general commitment to community service. At its eighth convention, the Legion noted that about a quarter of the men examined by the Selective Service System in 1917 were physically unfit for any military service. Speakers at national and department conventions urged local posts to organize "moral and athletic" activities in a generation beset by the excesses of the Jazz Age. At the seventh national convention, a consensus emerged that youth baseball would be the means to achieve both ends. According to the proceedings of the 1923 National Legion Convention, what would be known as Junior All-American Baseball "would afford the American Legion the best possible medium through which to teach the principles of Americanism. Under cloak of a sport code, we would teach more good citizenship during one year than would be possible in five years of direct appeal."

Junior baseball shortly proved to be one of the Legion's most enduring contributions to the nation. Legion lore says it was the brainchild of K.D. Munro of South Dakota, whose department introduced the idea at the 1924 convention. Several departments had their own leagues before that and the national organization encouraged others to do so for the coming year. In 1926, the Legion held a junior world series at the national convention in Philadelphia.

The new Commission was enthusiastic about the rapid growth of Legion baseball. "It has solved the problem of approach to the red-blooded American boy who has no time for preachments or studious application to the doctrines of good citizenship," stated the Commission. By 1928, more than 120,000 boys had joined teams.

In its early years, Legion baseball was deliberately political, designed to combat "subversive elements" in America. It was also viewed as a way to assimilate second- and third-generation immigrants into society. "Stub" Allison, the program's national director, informed the Americanism Commission that "You will catch them when they are just a bunch of clay in your hands." For youth more and more absorbed by idle amusements, traditional patriotic education would not be enough. "How can you teach Americanism with a pencil and paper? We need a manly and patriotic means of teaching teamwork in times of crisis. . . . When the gong rings again, as it did in 1917, maybe these little cookies will go in there and do their stuff."

The promotion of Legion baseball has always been lively. William Pencak's discussion of Legion baseball in *For God and Country* points out how significant baseball was for the Legion's Americanism activities. The leadership considered it to be "the greatest Americanizing influence on the young manhood of America." Baseball was simply the most prominent of the "hundreds of activities among [the] young and adults that are helping in these troubled times to keep the country on an even keel." The Legion promoted baseball to parents and schools as a vigorous complement to the civics taught in the classroom. It also provided a wholesome outlet for the excess exuberance of youth and a proven way of getting the boys to turn to the Legion for guidance instead of into pacifists, according to a 1944 testimonial by National Americanism Director Daniel Sowers. Because of their work with young men at an early age, Legionnaires would be "heroes to the boys growing up in the communities, and it is up to them to say what kind of citizens these boys shall grow up to be. The rising generation will eat out of their hands."

Such goals helped the program receive, from 1928–32, about $50,000 from the major baseball leagues, which quickly realized the benefit of a program that trained future ball players and promoted major league clubs as solid citizens in their own right. The financial impact of the Depression, however, forced professional baseball to curtail support for more than a decade. During this time, the Legion relied upon a variety of sources for support. In 1933, for example, the Legion's National Convention record shows that "Colonel Henry L. Doherty, noted engineer, scientist, financier, and philanthropist," gave $6,500 to Legion baseball and the Sporting Goods Manufacturing Association donated nearly $4,000. Other occasional contributors included major newspapers, businesses, and chambers of commerce.

The growth of the Pennsylvania program mirrored that of the national program. The department promoted sandlot baseball as a popular and easy execution of a post's civic and communal duty. Civic organizations such as the Rotary and Kiwanis clubs and church groups of all denominations contributed to Legion work. Many posts contributed more than their share of energy. Reading's Post #12 and Butler's Post #117 helped to field nine teams in 1929. In the same year, Hanover Post #14 and Kingston Post #395 organized five teams in their jurisdictions. Legionnaires in the initial efforts included Vincent A. Carrol, William Phillips, and Lucius M. Crumrine. Each encountered difficulties in coordinating statewide activities despite widespread enthusiasm. It was hard to enforce the age rule of various teams. Some would field post-high school athletes or even young professionals in an effort to win championships. This created suspicion and distrust among players, coaches, and organizers. The Pennsylvania program was also hurt by the untimely death of Barney Dreyfus of Pittsburgh's Liberty Post #5 in 1929. He had served as the high commissioner of Legion baseball in the state and was one of its most hard-working and enthusiastic proponents.

In 1932, after six years in which much infighting and indecision plagued Legion baseball in the state, the department called on the man who would lead the program for generations, George E. Bellis. At an informal meeting at the Stanfield Boys Club in Philadelphia, department Commander George Proesel and Adjutant James J. Deighan discussed youth activities in the city and state. Bellis had for several years worked with youth baseball and gymnastics teams sponsored by parochial schools in Philadelphia. They agreed to discuss the matter further at a gathering at the Department headquarters, then on South Third Street in Philadelphia. After surveying the problems of Legion baseball in the state, they agreed to investigate and report to a department committee on protests against the ineligibility of teams and other obstacles. In 1933, department Commander Paul H. Griffith appointed Bellis as secretary of the Baseball Committee. Bellis worked with Frank Stinger and Joe Schmidt, two of the founders of Legion baseball in Pennsylvania, to reform the program.

A native of Catasaqua, Bellis moved to the Philadelphia area in the 1930s. He was eager to work with youth. In his service in France, Bellis had organized YMCA activities for doughboys to relieve boredom and idleness. He later coached at Germantown Academy, assisted with the sports program at Philadelphia's Boys Clubs and helped with the physical education classes in fifty-two parochial schools in the area. In the tradition of the era, Bellis advocated "constructive Americanism" through thought and deed. A former quartermaster sergeant, Bellis was an experienced organizer. He also advocated that all boys, regardless of ability, be allowed to participate in Legion baseball. To him, sports was only a means to an end. The goal was to mold better citizens, not merely good athletes.

Bellis led the program for thirty-one years. As activities chairman of the Pennsylvania department, he also eventually directed youth basketball, bowling, and golf programs. It was his long association with youth baseball, however, that earned him greatest recognition. In 1934, Bellis officially succeeded Schmidt as the head of Legion baseball, involving 150 teams. In the following year, he persuaded Philadelphia A's manager Connie Mack to lend his name to the state's Legion program. Thereafter, Connie Mack baseball (and after 1953, Connie Mack basketball) was offered to all boys from fourteen to eighteen in Pennsylvania.

Bellis was always looking out for the youngsters. In 1937, he withdrew Pennsylvania from national competition because "national rules did not fit in with the program adopted by the department committee." Bellis wanted a longer season and a rule that would permit "youngsters who had been friends for many years to play on the same team and continue their friendship on the ball field." Pennsylvania didn't re-enter the national program until 1968. Bellis also constantly urged the local press to promote Legion baseball. From Scranton to Erie, the headlines of community newspapers read, "Sports as Curb on Crime Urged by the American Legion" and "Plan More Play Areas on

Vacant Lots; The American Legion Opens War to Check Crime Among Youth." During the off-season, Bellis and the Department Athletic Committee sponsored the first statewide basketball tournament in 1937, with 105 posts sponsoring 260 teams.

Legion baseball was boosted in 1940 when station KYW in Philadelphia agreed to broadcast a number of games. By 1950, there were more than 1,000 teams. Bellis traveled 50,000 miles a year keeping an eye on the operation. At the 26th department convention, he met for two hours with sports writers from Pittsburgh and Philadelphia as well as officials from the state's three major league teams. At the same time, however, Bellis expressed the fear that many of the problems of youth noticed after World War I had continued despite Legion efforts:

> The humiliating facts of the low physical condition of American youth today have been made known by the findings of the medical examiners in the Selective Service. That so many of our boys were unable to pass those tests is a shock to all of us. . . . The boy himself should not be blamed. Baseball today is at a crossroads. It is sad to admit that the interest in our national game has fallen away. . . . Let's all get in there and help put over this great program and put baseball where it belongs—first in the heart of the American boy."

Then came Legion baseball's darkest hour. Midget baseball, devoted to boys under twelve, emerged in 1950. Conceived in Ohio, the program quickly caught on with parents in the developing suburbs. Sponsors from local businesses and civic groups flocked to it, cutting in half the number of Legion teams and leagues. Bellis embarked on a massive effort to restore the prestige of Legion baseball. He preached that teenagers needed organized recreational activities as much as the little tykes. Bellis also noted the national concern for physical fitness and good health. Legionnaires and others were again brought into the circle of Legion baseball. In a little more than five years, Legion baseball had regained its stature.

In the depths of the Depression, "juvenile delinquency" became a serious social issue. National educators and leaders identified it as the main threat to America's future. The Legion had started its baseball program to give the older boy an outlet for activity. Bellis and other members of his committee had to bring this issue to the people of the state.

Pushed into the background by World War II and the Cold War, the issue of youth crime reappeared in the mid-1950s. Many adults voiced concern about rock and roll and other aspects of the new youth culture. Widespread affluence brought the additional challenge of filling many more leisure hours.

The Legion mobilized against juvenile delinquency in 1954. Approximately 300,000 American Legion members holding cards in 984 posts sponsored the new Jimmy Foxx Youth program. Foxx, a baseball Hall of Famer and former slugger with the Philadelphia Athletics, was to lead a group of twenty or more major leaguers on a tour of cities and towns. Only boys between twelve and eighteen would be invited by sponsoring groups to attend the meetings. Bellis said, "If we can get 200 kids in one room and have the ball players come before them, some good will rub off on maybe fifty of them who might otherwise go wrong." Foxx, who left his meat-distributing business in Miami to work on the project, wanted to keep it as simple and straightforward as possible. "I know about kids and ball players," Foxx later told a newspaper. "They will listen to a player before they will a minister and if only a little of what we tell them takes effect, we may eventually keep hundreds of American boys from going to jail." Over eight months, 10,000 boys from across the state heard the "Pennsylvania Caravan" of ball players endorsing the virtues of hard work, sacrifice, and perseverance. The idea originated with Roy Gregory, a Legionnaire from Bridgeport, Connecticut. He submitted it to baseball Commissioner Ford Frick and received his enthusiastic approval. Bellis soon said that "Pennsylvania will take the lead in this fine set-up and it is hoped to enlarge the program to a national scale within the next year." Those most active in the initial stages of the project included Daniel Shaub, Milton Moore, Leon Duckworth, Dr. Almo Sebastianelli, and Ed Hoak. Such Legion-sponsored caravans remained popular in the state until the late 1960s.

Major league teams in the state resumed their support of Legion baseball after World War II. In the summer of 1953, Legionnaires in eastern Pennsylvania participated in the sixth annual city championship game between the two Philadelphia major league teams, the Athletics and the Phillies, at Connie

Mack Stadium. Sponsored by the Junior Baseball Federation, the game helped raise money to buy bats, balls, gloves, and other equipment for 30,000 youngsters who played sandlot baseball. Legion posts, in conjunction with the Sandlot Sports Association and Police Athletic Leagues, reached thousands of youngsters annually. The theme of 1953, for example, was "Take a Boy to a Ballgame." Legionnaires were asked not only to contribute money but to take several children, usually orphans, to a game.

Many young Legion baseball players went on to the major leagues. In 1962, for instance, Howie Podell, who had played in Pottstown, went on to the Milwaukee Braves. Bob Morehead of Lemoyne went to the New York Mets. Doug Clemens of McKeesport went to the St. Louis Cardinals. Joe Bonikowski, a member of the Corporal John Loudenslager Post #366 of Philadelphia, whose team was the first from Philadelphia in more than thirty years to reach the state finals and win the championship, became a member of the Minnesota Twins. Hundreds of others signed minor league contracts. Pennsylvania also contributed more than its share of umpires over the years. In 1962, Cal Hubbard, supervisor of American League umpires and who began his career in Legion baseball, remained on the Legion advisory staff along with ten other umpires from the two major leagues.

That same year, as usual, the Pennsylvania Legion sponsored a number of contact programs between youngsters and the major leagues. Two clinics were conducted through the cooperation of Joe Brown, then general manager of the Pittsburgh Pirates, and John Quinn, general manager of the Philadelphia Phillies. The first was held on April 21, with more than 1,100 coaches and players from the Legion's Western District, A Pittsburgh journalist called it the largest baseball clinic in the history of baseball. Danny Murtaugh, the Pirates manager, participated, as did several players and all his coaches. In the afternoon, Legion coaches and players watched the Pirates play the Mets. A similar clinic was held for 500 coaches and players from the eastern and central districts by the Phillies under the guidance of R.R.M. Carpenter and Phillies manager John Quinn.

Legion baseball was also promoted through American Legion Days organized by major league clubs and department officials.

On Saturday, June 16, 1962, in Pittsburgh, Commander George F. Bruno, his staff, and the Activities Committee visited the Pirates and presented awards to Jimmy Dykes, a coach for the Milwaukee Braves who had been a member of the department advisory staff since 1932; Howie Podell, a recent Legion player from Pottstown; and Warren Spahn, the eventual Hall of Fame pitcher, who received the Connie Mack 1962 Player Award. Also honored were two former members of the Swissvale team: Jack Berger, publicity director of the Pirates, and Charles Muse, a scout with a number of teams, including the Pirates.

From 1932–46, the department sponsored the Legion baseball program. In 1946, Commander James P. Murray and Adjutant Edward A. Linsky re-organized the Activities Committee and gave it additional funding. It was then responsible for all athletic programs. By the postwar period, these included two basketball divisions, the Pee-Wee and the Knee-High. Ed Hoak, post commander in Manor and a future adjutant and department commander, helped pioneer Knee-High (for ten- to fourteen-year-olds) basketball in the central part of the state. The concerns of young women were not ignored. Under the sponsorship of the Helen Fairchild post, the Nurses' Basketball League was organized among the sixteen hospitals in Philadelphia; Montgomery County, Pennsylvania; and Camden, New Jersey. The league was strictly for student nurses and was the only one of its kind in the country. Golf tournaments, bowling leagues, shooting competitions, and touch football leagues were regular Legion-sponsored activities. As activities chairman, Bellis was in charge of Connie Mack baseball for boys from fourteen to sixteen, Legion Baseball for boys sixteen to eighteen, and statewide Pee-Wee and Knee-High basketball playoffs. He also helped to start annual Legion state bowling and golf tournaments.

During Bellis's tenure, 100 young men reached the major leagues. Just before his retirement in 1965, he gave his hypothetical "all-star" team of former Keystone Legion players: The outfield consisted of Del Ennis, Stan Musial, and Elmer Valo. Mickey Vernon was at third base, Nellie Fox at shortstop, Dick Groat at second base, and Whitney Kurowski at first. Roy Campanella, the Dodgers star whose career was tragically cut short by illness, was catcher. The pitching rotation was filled by Ken Raffensberger, Curt Simmons, and Gary Peters. Bellis enjoyed a brief retirement before succumbing to illness and dying at his home in Wyndmoor, a suburb of Philadelphia, at age sixty-eight.

Players old and young quickly acknowledged the role of Bellis and the Legion in shaping their careers. Many attended a memorial service for Bellis. The national media also covered Legion baseball in Pennsylvania in the postwar years. Campanella credited Bellis and the John Loudenslager Post of Philadelphia for having given him a start in baseball. A pictorial of him and the post was published in *Time* magazine in 1955. In an article in the *Saturday Evening Post* in the same year, Fox lauded Bellis and the St. Thomas Post in the Chambersburg area for "setting him on the right road." Similar stories appeared on countless former Legion players in the three decades following Bellis's time. More than anything, the continued strength and vitality of the program, which now attracts nearly 500,000 boys, is an enduring testimony to Bellis and the other founders.

Besides baseball, the Pennsylvania Legion sponsors Boy Scout troops across the state. Since the goals of Scouting and Legion youth work are quite close, it makes sense for the organizations to work together. Legionnaires serve as Scout leaders and aid religious groups and others in the formation of troops.

The Legion also struck out on its own. Beginning in 1936, the Pennsylvania department organized a program to teach the rights and duties of citizenship to young men. Local posts would screen and recruit sophomores and juniors in high school according to their interest and ability in civics. The program was called Boys State in Pennsylvania and elsewhere. The first year, "Keystone Boys' Camp" (the name was later changed to the more conventional term) was held at Mount Gretna. The next year and for a long time it was held at Indiantown Gap. The program was suspended during World War II and resumed at Indiantown Gap in 1946. In 1950, the camp was transferred to Lock Haven State Teachers' College. Since the 1960s, the site for Boys' State has been rotated among locations such as Harrisburg, Millersville, and Quakertown to ensure greater access for participants coming from all over the state. From the start, an average of 500 representatives who have won Legion school awards have met to learn and exercise the techniques of government. The Legion combines classroom work with a range of other activities. According to a publicity brochure sent to parents, organizers reasoned that "if the American Legion obtains the confidence of our boys, [they] will stand by the principles of the Legion."

For a time, the program was extended to young women as well. The first Keystone Girls' Camp, organized by the Auxiliary, was held at Gettysburg from June 22 to July 2, 1940. Attended by 150 girls, it was organized along the lines of the Boys' Camp with course in more appropriate for young women. The program was discontinued because of financial constraints after World War II and never resumed.

Lock Haven State Teachers College was the site of the 1953 Keystone Boys' State, attended by about 240 boys. The goal was to train the statesmen and leaders of the future. Tom E. Williams, the program director in the 1950s, said, "It is not a camp of entertainment . . . it is not a camp for the problem boy. It is a camp in which the youth of our country, preferably those who have a year left in high school, are trained in the responsibilities of being an American citizen and the principles of democracy."

The participants were divided into "Conservative" and "National" parties. Dormitories were divided and each was considered a "state." The goal was to teach participants direct democracy, the art of persuasion, and other electoral procedures.

Correspondingly, mayors, legislators, and finally governors were elected by each party's "constituents." They were gathered and instructed in their duties. Each party caucused, debates were organized between opposing candidates, and overall elections were held. The new public servants had to formulate a budget and listen to the voters' complaints. In short, Boys' State was organized to be a microcosm of practical Americanism and elected government. "In that short time," a future legislator from Erie remembered, "I learned more about the pressures of government than all the classroom instruction in the world could have taught me."

The Legion also organized physical and moral education. Afternoons were devoted to hiking, swimming, soccer, softball, and volleyball. Teams were chosen from both parties to avoid polarizing all activities. In the evening, light educational sessions were held featuring speakers from military academies and the State Fish and Game Commission. Films such as "Knute Rockne: All-American," "The Babe Ruth Story," and "The Pride of the Yankees" were screened.

The success of the Keystone Boys' State was seen years later. The first generation of Boys' State, for example, produced an array of public servants, professionals, and men from all walks of life who made a real impact on their communities. Among them was Jack Fritz of Johnstown, Boys' State governor in 1937. He served in the Navy in World War II, graduated from Pennsylvania State University, and became a notable lawyer in New Jersey. Jack Morgan, governor in 1938 and formerly of Scranton, served in World War II and Korea and became a civil engineer in Baltimore. Another participant in the 1938 camp went on to Boys' Nation and became a local councilman in California.

For several reasons, attendance at the annual camps has fluctuated greatly over the years, though they remain a central part of the Legion's youth program. Generations have come and gone, but the principles of instruction and goals have remained the same.

The Keystone Legion was also involved in a nationwide endeavor, the Sons of the American Legion, in which the male descendants of Legion members were organized into an auxiliary. The goal was to transmit the ideas and values of the Legion to posterity. In the manner of the women's Auxiliary, the Sons of the American Legion was chartered in 1933 to carry out local community service and patriotic work. "Our sons are logical candidates to succeed us," noted a post commander from Lebanon, "and it is our duty to see that they are trained, not only in the principles and ideals, but also in the actual program, of the parent organization." Legionnaires such as the first chairman of the S.A.L. organizing committee, Edwin B. Yeich, faced a tough challenge in persuading many Legion posts to organize "squadrons" for the new group. The organization of S.A.L squadrons was considered too time-consuming and distracting by some post commanders. Yeich helped to write a pamphlet, "A Program for the Sons of the Legion, Department of Pennsylvania." It presented the S.A.L.'s philosophy and a plan for "organizing and administering the individual squadron, and a suggested list of activities for its members." This pamphlet was supplemented throughout the year by bulletins, letters, and personal visits. By the late 1930s, state S.A.L. membership varied between 6,000 and 9,000, with an average of 364 squadrons reporting in yearly. Squadrons were given names such as Fort Pitt or Fort Washington to emphasize the military heritage of the nation and give young men something to identify with. Sons of Legionnaires were also attracted by the special activities: color guards, drill teams, glee clubs, and ritual teams. The report at the 1938 department convention said, "Musical organizations seem to be a predominant feature, with a great many bugle corps and a few bands and orchestras." Outdoor activities also were popular. Some squadrons held summer camps, hiking parties, and picnics. In athletics, "baseball and basketball predominate, although softball, boxing, wrestling, and bowling have their share of participants," and "a great many rifle clubs have been formed among the boys."

The significance of the Keystone S.A.L. was soon seen when the nation was engulfed in World War II. Many members served in the military and afterward joined the Legion. One was Edward McCoy (1922–81), son of Joseph McCoy, a former doughboy and a long-time Legionnaire from a post in Bradford. McCoy participated in a squadron that emphasized athletic training and the responsible use of weapons; he also played Legion baseball and attended the Boys' State camp in 1939. Enlisting (as his father did) in the Army in 1941, he served in North Africa and the European theater. McCoy earned the Bronze Star in 1944, was honorably discharged in 1945, and returned to the Bradford area. He joined his father's post and served as post adjutant and commander over three decades of Legion membership. In an interview, McCoy credited his participation in Legion youth activities with "setting him on the straight and narrow" from an early boyhood of hard times. "Legion baseball and camping [often sponsored by the S.A.L.] was the only thing going for young men of my age. Without them, who knows what I would've gotten into?"

After languishing from the end of World War II to the 1980s, Sons of the American Legion has made a comeback. There are now department-wide "detachments" or conventions on a regular basis. The national adjutant called the Pennsylvania contingent the fastest growing in the country. It received the Arthur D. Houghton Award at the national convention in Phoenix, Arizona, in 1992 for the greatest percentage increase over the previous year's membership. More than 3,000 men of all ages are now enrolled in about 160 squadrons. S.A.L. drill teams and rifle squads have become a vital part of post life in many areas. The state's success was attributed by John Curley Sieger, chairman of its S.A.L., to the theme "We Are Family" and the group's campaign to preserve family traditions.

In 1991, Legion baseball was thriving in Pennsylvania. Between $3 million and $5 million a year was being spent on the seventy-five teams in the Junior League (thirteen- to fifteen-year-olds) and the 490 or so teams for the older teens. More than 10,000 boys and girls played Legion baseball that summer. Girls had been a common sight; one was among the starting nine on the 1991 championship team from Beaver Falls. The sheer numbers made Pennsylvania's program the largest in Legion baseball (Minnesota was a distant second with 280 teams in 1991). The 1991 major league draft selected forty-four amateurs from Pennsylvania; forty-one had played Legion baseball at one stage.

In all, the youth programs serve the state, members, and their children. They consistently reflect well on the Legion. By their words and actions, George Bellis and his successors enhanced the Legion's positive force in the state.

BIBLIOGRAPHICAL
ESSAY

I used two main archival sources in the research and writing of this project. The Pennsylvania department's headquarters in Wormleysburg provided several archival files on key issues of recent interest (Legionnaires' disease, Agent Orange, the Panama Canal controversy) as well as the records of long-time Adjutant Edward Hoak. I interviewed more than twenty Legionniares, including Mr. Hoak, Department Commanders Stanley Reinhard, Tom Cammarota, Dominic DiFrancesco, John Stay, and many others. Harry V. Klein of Sunbury arranged a number of these interviews and devoted much of his time and energy to the completion of the project.

The second archival source was the American Legion Archives and Library at the headquarters in Indianapolis. The Legion Library has files on all departments; I used the Pennsylvania file extensively, along with several manuscript collections relating to the Pennsylvania department, such as "Americanism" and "Veterans Administration." The library houses a microfilm collection that contains the complete department convention proceedings as well as the recorded minutes of department Executive Committee meetings. I used these files in addition to the microfilmed copies of the various post newspapers, the *Adjutant's Newsletter* and the *Pennsylvania Legionniare*. I appreciate the assistance of Joseph J. Hovish and his staff, without which this book could not have been completed.

In addition to the primary research collections, several monographs and articles were indispensable in the formation of certain chapters. Chapter 1 could not have been written without the background found in John La and William Pencak's *For God and Country: The American Legion, 1919–1941* (Boston, 1989). The book provided a good start on an examination of the American Legion during the 1930s and 1940s, as well as background on the Legion and youth activities. Gordon Thomas and Max Morgan-Witts's *Anatomy of an Epidemic* (New York, 1982), perhaps the only complete account of the outbreak of Legionnaires' disease, provided a good deal of information on the subject. A special commemorative article by Larry Lewis in the July 21, 1991, editon of the *Philadelphia Inquirer* was also invaluable in the writing of that chapter. Finally, Thomas A. Rumer's *The American Legion: An Official History, 1919–1989* was a solid model for the research and writing of this subject.

APPENDICES

DEPARTMENT COMMANDERS

1919	William G. Murdock, Milton
1919–20	George F. Tyler, Philadelphia
1920–21	David J. Davis, Scranton
1921–22	Joseph H. Thompson, Beaver Falls
1922–23	William B. Healey, Wilkes-Barre
1923–24	J. Leo Collins, East Pittsburgh
1924–25	J. Mitchell Chase, Clearfield
1925–26	L. McK. Crumrine, Washington
1926–27	Robert M. Vail, Kingston
1927–28	E. E. Hollenback, Philadelphia
1928–29	Charles A. Gebert, Tamaqua
1929–30	Frank L. Pinola, Wilkes-Barre
1930–31	Charles I. Engard, Philadelphia
1931–32	George J. Proesl, DuBois
1932–33	Paul H. Griffith, Uniontown
1933–34	Otto F. Messner, Lancaster
1934–35	J. Ernest Isherwood, Waynesburg
1935–36	John B. McDade, Scranton
1936–37	Walter J. Kress, Harrisburg
1937–38	William F. Smith, Punxsutawney
1938–39	Frank E. Gwynn, Allentown
1939–40	Edward R. Stirling, Vandergrift
1940–41	Charles S. Cook, West Pittston
1941–42	I. G. Gordon Forster, Philadelphia
1942–43	Daniel C. Hartbauer, Pittsburgh
1943–44	Frank X. Murray, Scranton
1944–45	William J. Rhoads, Rutledge
1945–46	James Murray, Forest City
1946–47	Clyde E. Rankin, Philadelphia
1947–48	William L. Windsor, Harrisburg
1948–49	Lawrence Trainor, Duquesne
1949–50	Walter E. Alessandroni, Philadelphia
1950–51	Joseph S. McCracken, Kingston
1951–52	Jack R. Dodson, Greensburg
1952–53	Herbert M. Walker, Langhorne
1953–54	Paul R. Selecky, Wilkes-Barre
1954–55	Sherman W. Mason, Jeannette
1955–56	John F. Stay, Philadelphia
1956–57	Joseph P. Gavenois, Harrisburg

1957–58	John W. Collins, Connellsville
1958–59	Paul E. Walters, Pine Grove
1959–60	William T. Malone, Scranton
1960–61	Edward T. Hoak, Manor
1961–62	George F. Bruno, Bethlehem
1962–63	Louis J. Greco, Wyoming
1963–64	Regis F. Cusick, Pittsburgh
1964–65	Monroe R. Bethman, Doylestown
1965–66	Harry V. Klein, Sunbury
1966–67	Joseph I. Harshman, Fredericktown
1967–68	Theodore F. Foedisch, Philadelphia
1968–69	John E. Gilbert, Fredericksburg
1969–70	Henry R. Woods, Pittsburgh
1970–71	E. Thomas Cammarota, North Wales
1971–72	William G. Kays, Dunmore
1972–73	David T. Minto, Sr., Trafford
1973–74	Don H. Jeffrey, Philadelphia
1974–75	Richard W. Snyder, Williamsport
1975–76	John E. Titus, Jefferson
1976–77	Joseph V. Adams, Cheltenham
1977–78	Eugene C. Eichelberger, St. Thomas
1978–79	Stephen J. Mikosky, Jeannette
1979–80	John Zweisdak, Allentown
1980–81	Ernest P. Zserai, Jonestown
1981–82	Victor T. Raia, Altoona
1982–83	F. Rodney Loper, West Chester
1983–84	Nello Carozzoni, Wilkes-Barre
1984–85	L. G. Smith, Latrobe
1985–86	Stanley W. Reinhard, Jr., Coplay
1986–87	Dominic D. DiFrancesco, Middletown
1987–88	Ronald F. Conley, Pittsburgh
1988–89	Al Pirolli, Philadelphia
1989–90	Frederick W. Wagner, Hummelstown
1990–91	R. Raymond Lenz, Cresson
1991–92	Joseph R. Chase, Hatboro
1992–93	Edwin Markiewicz, Nanticoke

DEPARTMENT VICE COMMANDERS

1919–20   Lyell Spangel, Williamsport
Alexander McLaughlin, Pittsburgh
H. C. Blank, Allentown

1920–21   C. C. McLain, Indiana
David B. Simpson, Philadelphia
Maurice E. Finney, Harrisburg

1921–22   Francis A. Lewis, Philadelphia
Mark T. Milnor, Harrisburg
L. McK. Crumrine, Washington

1922–23   Dr. S. A. Baltz, Uniontown
John M. Groff, Lancaster
Jesse M. Kline, Scranton

1923–24   Frank L. Pinola, Wilkes-Barre
Dr. W. E. Raken, Philadelphia
Paul Kuhn, Altoona

1924–25   Earl A. Ziegenfus, Bethlehem
Dr. J. J. Bellas, Lansford
Henry S. Coshey, Jr., Greensburg

1925–26   Dr. E. J. Williams, Huntingdon
Jacob F. Miller II, Hatboro
Dr. C. A. Rogers, Freeport

1926–27   Harry B. Bunting, Pittsburgh
Daniel B. Strickler, Lancaster
A. W. Sheasley, Williamsport

1927–28   Ray E. Taylor, Harrisburg
Bernard L. Keenan, Johnsonburg
Robert J. W. Neall, Lansdowne

1928–29   Dr. Ralph B. McCord, North East
Harvey R. Bowman, Williamsport
Roy B. Sheetz, Mount Joy

1929–30   Ben Howarth, Willow Grove
John J. Deller, Wilmerding
Joseph D. Fox, Milton

1930–31	Sidney B. Martin, West Pittston George J. Proesl, DuBois Robert J. Hanna, Philadelphia
1931–32	Frank A. Kanter, Philadelphia Charles R. Schweizer, Honesdale Paul H. Griffith, Uniontown
1932–33	George H. Ervin, Waynesboro Otto F. Messner, Lancaster John G. Watson, Pittsburgh
1933–34	J. Ernest Isherwood, Waynesburg W. Klein, Shamokin Dam A. B. Kehr, Philadelphia
1934–35	Paul Dague, Downingtown John Harrison, Archbald Carl Hoffman, Somerset
1935–36	William F. Smith, Punxsutawney Harry K. Stinger, Philadelphia Hobart Hopkins, New Cumberland
1936–37	Mark L. Tingley, Blossburg James M. Donohue, Coaldale Edward R. Stirling, Vandergrift
1937–38	Frank E. Gwynn, Allentown Kenneth J. Guest, Plymouth Silas Waddell, Pittsburgh
1938–39	Wilbur Brown, Waynesboro Guy Wadlinger, New Castle Clayton Williams, Lansford
1939–40	Jospeh I. Finnerty, Philadelphia Dan McKinney, Sunbury Henry Brown, Meadville
1940–41	Dan C. Hartbauer, Pittsburgh William J. Rhoads, Rutledge James P. Murray, Forest City

1941–42	Abe Shelley, Steelton Louis Nagy, Monongahela Paul R. Sine, Perkasie
1942–43	Richard White, Philadelphia Michael Onze, Olyphant M. R. Tibby, Punxsutawney
1943–44	Robert C. Malcolm, Curtisville Charles R. McCann, Reading Louis H. Harris, Lewisburg
1944–45	Al C. Nichols, Lock Haven Joseph Straub, Johnstown Homer Sarge, Pine Grove
1945–46	Clyde Rankin, Philadelphia John Stoup, Waynesburg William Windsor, Harrisburg
1946–47	Lawrence Trainor, Duquesne Joseph MacCracken, Kingston Dixie Dryden, Chester
1947–48	Thomas Brown, Philadelphia Al Gillette, Oil City Milt Moore, Sunbury
1948–49	Emory Rockwell, Wellsboro Jackson R. Dodson, Greensburg Elmer Leddon, Willow Grove
1949–50	Warren McCarty, Claysburg Lewis M. Krebs, Port Carbon James W. Heffernan, York
1950–51	Edwin H. Strickler, Lansford Paul Ord, Scranton Edward G. Petrillo, Erie
1951–52	William Hetherington, Selinsgrove George C. Deitrich, Pittsburgh Thomas Plummer, Paoli

1952–53	John Collins, Connellsville
	John Stay, Philadelphia
	Charles Miller, Hawley
1953–54	Fred H. E. Dorney, Allentown
	Joseph J. Huss, Hummelstown
	Sherman Mason, Jeannette
1954–55	Robert O. Crawford, Butler
	Charles A. Mentzer, New Holland
	Oscar Renfer, West Pittston
1955–56	Paul Walters, Pine Grove
	Joseph Gavenonis, Harrisburg
	Frederick Morley, Barnesboro
1956–57	Owen A. Johnson, Jersey Shore
	J. Edward Herring, Somerset
	Thomas Kane, Philadelphia
1957–58	Edward Hoak, Manor
	George F. Bruno, Bethlehem
	Earl Sollenberger, York
1958–59	Walter Mason, Havertown
	Joseph P. Graham, Scranton
	Regis F. Cusick, Jr., Pittsburgh
1959–60	J. LeRoy Cumbler, Newport
	Kenneth Davis, Homer City
	Monroe R. Bethman, Doylestown
1960–61	Joseph I. Harshman, Fredericktown
	Daniel A. Kimmel, Tower City
	George Miller, Wyalusing
1961–62	Theodore F. Foedisch, Philadelphia
	J. Ben Dubson, Palmyra
	William A. Comoroda, Pittsburgh
1962–63	Thomas W. O'Connor, Spring City
	John R. Gallagher, Freeland
	A. John Garritano, Altoona

1963–64   John Dean, Philadelphia
Chester Duchman, Montandon
George D. Yorns, Beaver

1964–65   Robert F. Ertwine, Ringtown
Hugh Conningham, Blossburg
David Minto, Trafford

1965–66   Charles C. Harrison, St. Thomas
John C. Mann, Clearfield
Donald W. McPherson, Hellertown

1966–67   Warren Morgan, Sharon
H. Richard Francis, Sharon Hill
William Kays, Dunmore

1967–68   Joseph Adams, Cheltenham
Elmer L. Hafer, Lewisburg
Henry R. Woods, Pittsburgh

1968–69   Daniel C. Deobold, Brackney
Robert F. Bittner, Meyersdale
E. Thomas Cammarota, Philadelphia

1969–70   Dom Presto, Baden
Edward C. Kennedy, Summit Hill
Eugene R. Buggy, Lykens

1970–71   Fred Pellegrino, Coplay
Nello Carozzoni, Wilkes-Barre
John E. Titus, Jefferson

1971–72   Robert Bastian, Milton
Stephen J. Mikosky, Jeannette
Donald H. Jeffery, Philadelphia

1972–73   Robert L. Coughlin, McKeesport
Albert B. Hall, Jr., Elkins Park
Richard W. Snyder, Williamsport

1973–74   Joseph Kline, Tamaqua
Eugene C. Eichelberger, Thomas
Victor T. Raia, Altoona

1974–75	William C. Hartsough, Lancaster John J. Dunn, Sr., Scranton Dr. A. Hal Reede, State College
1975–76	Al Pirolli, Philadelphia Chester Peterson, Enola Lee A. Shaw, Pittsburgh
1976–77	John J. Sheleman, Dushore Frank Parry, Charleroi Dawson Brown, Lehighton
1977–78	Ernest P. Zserai, Jonestown Frank Spreha, Pittsburgh John Zweisdak, Allentown
1978–79	Peter Baller, Plains Peter Standish, Mars F. Rodney Loper, West Chester
1979–80	Louise Emond, Hatboro Robert Joe, New Columbia Jack Haines, Monroeville
1980–81	Kenneth Miller, Pine Grove Andrew Condo, East Williamsport Victor Straub, St. Mary's
1981–82	Stanley W. Reinhard, Jr., Coplay Dale Sprenkle, Dallastown L. G. Smith, Latrobe
1982–83	Mario Antonucci, Hiller Anthony R. Gallo, Fort Washington Robert E. Reilly, Scranton
1983–84	Jeffrey L. Seler, McClure John Bowen, Philadelphia Ron Conley, Pittsburgh
1984–85	Herman R. Smeltz, East Stroudsburg Robert E. Yeager, DuBois Joseph H. Baker, Wyalusing

1985–86   Joseph F. Chase, Philadelphia
Frederick W. Wagner, Hummelstown
R. Raymond Lenz, Cresson

1986–87   Edwin Markiewicz, Nanticoke
Frank Tucci, Farrell
Joseph A. Palermo, Ambler

1987–88   John J. King, DuBois
Dr. James D. Shafer, East Stroudsburg
Donald V. Thomas, Bloomsburg

1988–89   Thomas J. Veney, Philadelphia
Bradley H. Oechler, Williamsport
Charles G. Pollacci, Charleroi

1989–90   Joseph V. Glazier, Quakertown
Jasper Stouffer, Chambersburg
James Comiskey, Pittsburgh

1990–91   James Gallagher, Newtown Square
Arlington Phillips, Jr., Scranton
Frank Chinnici, Irwin

1991–92   Joseph Socha, Philadelphia
Ernest Reinninger, Selinsgrove
Frank Shaffer, Six Mile Run

1992–93   Robert Shalala, Philadelphia
Richard Ayers, Meshoppen
Clare Blakeslee, Union City

DEPARTMENT ADJUTANTS

1920	Gilliam Aertsen, Jr., Philadelphia
1920–21	William G. Murdock, Milton
1921–23	Gilbert Jacoboski, Philadelphia
1923–35	James J. Deighan
1935–52	Edward A. Linsky, Philadelphia
1953–63	Daniel W. Shaub, Harrisburg
1963–91	Edward T. Hoak, Manor
1991	Stanley W. Reinhard, Jr., Coplay

NATIONAL COMMANDERS

1919	Franklin D'Olier, Philadelphia
1946	Paul H. Griffith, Uniontown
1991	Dominic D. DiFrancesco, Middletown

NATIONAL VICE COMMANDERS

1923–24	William B. Healey, Wilkes-Barre
1925–26	Vincent A. Carroll, Philadelphia
1929–30	Frank Scholbe, Jr., Wyncote
1940–41	Edward R. Stirling, Greensburg
1948–49	Walter E. Allessandroni, Philadelphia
1953–54	Herbert M. Walker, Langhorne
1956–57	John F. Stay, Philadelphia
1958–59	John W. Collins, Connellsville
1961–62	Edward T. Hoak, Manor
1966–67	Harry T. Klein, Jr., Sunbury
1970–71	John E. Gilbert, Fredericksburg
1974–75	Don H. Jeffery, Philadelphia
1980–81	Dr. Almo J. Sebastianelli, Jessup
1984–85	Stephen J. Mikosky, Jeannette
1992–93	Joseph V. Adams, Cheltenham

NATIONAL CHAPLAINS

1926–27   Reverend Father Joseph L. N. Wolfe, Philadelphia
1967–68   Reverend Father Edward P. Nolan, Mountaintop

NATIONAL EXECUTIVE COMMITTEEMEN

1919   Franklin D'Olier, Philadelphia
1920   General A. J. Logan, Pittsburgh
1921–22   Joseph H. Thompson, Beaver Falls
1922–23   William B. Healey, Wilkes-Barre
1923–27   J. Leo Collins, East Pittsburgh
1927–30   L. McK. Crumrine, Washington
1930–32   Charles A. Gebert, Tamaqua
1932–37   Vincent A. Carroll, Philadelphia
1937–38   J. Guy Griffith, New Kensington
1942–51   Harry K. Stinger, Philadelphia
1952–53   William L. Windsor, Harrisburg
1954–65   Walter E. Alessandroni, Philadelphia
1966–72   Daniel A. Drew, Pittsburgh
1963–74   E. Thomas Cammarota, Philadelphia
1975–80   Dr. Almo J. Sebastianelli, Jessup
1981–85   Stephen J. Mikosky, Jeannette
1985–86   Dominic DiFrancesco, Middletown
1987–92   Joseph V. Adams, Cheltenham
1992   Ronald F. Conley, Pittsburgh

ALTERNATE NATIONAL EXECUTIVE COMMITTEEMEN

1920	George F. Tyler, Fort Washington
1920–22	William E. Murdock, Milton
1922–23	Gilbert Jacobosky, Wilkes-Barre
1923–24	Frank L. Pinola, Wilkes-Barre
1924–26	J. Mitchell Chase, Clearfield
1926–27	L. McK. Crumrine, Washington
1927–30	Daniel B. Strickler, Lancaster
1930–34	Miss Mary Welsh, Pittsburgh
1934–37	J. Guy Griffith, New Kensington
1937–42	Harry K. Stinger, Philadelphia
1942–43	Michael Markowitz, Swoyerville
1944–47	Robert C. Malcolm, Curtisville
1948–51	William L. Windsor, Harrisburg
1952–53	Edward C. Petrillo, Erie
1954–57	James M. Donohue, Coaldale
1958–62	John J. Antonini, Ridgway
1963–66	Daniel A. Drew, Pittsburgh
1966–68	George F. Bruno, Bethlehem
1969–72	Dr. Almo J. Sebastianelli, Jessup
1973–74	John E. Gilbert, Fredericksburg
1975–78	Stephen J. Mikosky, Jeannette
1978–80	William Gormley, Philadelphia
1981–84	Dominic DiFrancesco, Middletown
1985–86	Joseph V. Adams, Cheltenham
1987–88	L. G. Smith, Latrobe
1988–92	Ronald F. Conley, Pittsburgh
1992	Alfred Pirolli, Philadelphia

FIRST DISTRICT COMMANDERS
PHILADELPHIA COUNTY

1919	Edward G. Simonson
	Howard G. Buck
	J. H. Geise
	A. N. Sherman
1920	Thomas J. Moore
1921	I. G. Gordon Forster
1922	Dr. William E. Raken
1923	Glenn Clark
1924–25	William L. Jenkins
1926–29	Walter E. Lorman
1930–33	Ella Tomlinson
1934–35	William R. Graham
1935	Florence E. Wagner
1936–37	John J. McHenry
1938–39	James Falvey
1940–41	Anna Brice
1942–43	James Medlen
1944–45	Clark Stewart
1946–47	Joseph Cuneo
1948–49	James Medlen
1950–51	Joseph Moss
1952–53	William E. Hill
1954–55	Anthony Croce
1956–57	Santo A. Cannon
1958–59	William B. Robertson
1960–61	John Dean
1962–63	George W. Johnson
1964–65	Alfred Pirolli
1966	J. Edward Mattis, Jr.
1967	Alfred Priolli
1968–69	Domenic D'Alonzo
1970–71	Anna M. Harkins
1972–73	Alfred Pirolli
1974–75	Joseph F. Glassey
1976–77	Charles McAleer
1978–79	Joseph F. Chase
1980–81	Robert Bundy

District Realigned

SECOND DISTRICT COMMANDERS
PHILADELPHIA COUNTY

1919	George W. Carr	Joseph B. McCall, Jr.
	Otto R. Heiligman	George F. Tyler
	LeRoy Richards	Charles J. Biddle
	Samuel H. Jones	Michael Saxe
	Joseph I. McNichol	John W. Geary
	Charles Weinburg	Franklin D'Olier
	Charles B. White	A. Nevin Detrich
	I. G. Gordon Forster	Edgar W. Baird
	G. Aersten, Jr.	

1920	Thomas J. Moore
1921	I. G. Gordon Forster
1922	Dr. William E. Raken
1923	William H. DuBarry
1924–28	Louis McGill
1929–32	Fabian Levy
1933–34	William L. Jenkins
1935–36	John J. Haley
1937–38	Harry J. Martin
1939–40	Richard White
1941–42	J. F. O'Connor
1943–44	Leslie B. Adams
1945–46	Samuel J. C. Greene
1947–48	Walter L. Mason
1949–50	Joseph Riddle
1951–52	Marjorie Slocum
1953–54	Alvin J. Herr
1955–56	August Bendler
1957–58	Albert Dangel
1959–60	Christian F. Sandstrom
1961–62	Karl G. Ley, Jr.
1963–64	Louis Newman
1965–66	Edward F. Duross
1967–68	Edward J. Osowiecki
1969–70	William Mingle
1971–72	James D'Angelo
1973–74	Lewis MacClain

1975–76	Kazimierz Wilkowski
1977–78	Salvatore A. Aiello
1979–80	Catherine T. Cool
1981–82	William Lofton
1983–84	Viola Lewandowski
1985–86	Samuel W. Jefferson
1987–88	Robert D. Shalala
1989–90	Siegfried Honig
1990–91	James D. B. Weiss, Jr.
1991–93	Siegfried Honig

THIRD DISTRICT COMMANDERS
PHILADELPHIA COUNTY

1919	George Nofer
	Harry Taggart
	A. Knox
1920	Thomas J. Moore
1921	I. G. Gordon Forster
1922	Dr. William E. Raken
1923–25	William L. Charr
1926–27	William A. Johnson
1928–29	William L. Charr
1930–31	William H. Bertolet, Jr.
1932–35	Dr. J. Coscarello
1936–37	Fred Meyers
1938–39	James Lance
1940–41	William Power
1942–43	John Masciautonis
1944–45	Rushin Johnson
1946–47	Fred Myers
1948–49	Harry R. Fox
1950–51	Daniel Quinn
1952–53	Paul Tranchitella
1954–55	William E. Weber
1956	Raymond Gogolski
1957	Joseph Bongiovanni
1958–59	Arthur P. Wonhart
1960–61	Albert DelConte
1962–63	John Bautz
1964–65	Louis Tentarelli
1966–67	George A. Graeff
1968–69	Michael Lalli
1970–71	Elmer Confair
1972–73	James Payne
1974–75	Charles Burns
1976	Mike Lalli

District Realigned

FOURTH DISTRICT COMMANDERS
PHILADELPHIA COUNTY

1919	James O'Donnell
	Adelbert Hoerger
	M. Penny
1920	Thomas J. Moore
1921	I. G. Gordon Forster
1922	Dr. William E. Raken
1923	Glendon Tongue
1924–26	Dr. William E. Raken
1927	Stover L. Detweiler
1928	Joel Kauffman
1929–30	Norman Gotwals
1931	Arthur Taylor
1932	Herman N. Schwartz
1933	Herman N. Schwartz/Sam Coplin
1934	Sam Coplin
1935–36	James J. McGuigan
1937–38	Craig Herbert
1939–40	Norman Morell
1941–42	Meyer Abrams
1943–44	James J. Dunphy
1945–46	John J. Collins
1947	Michael Bachmeyer
1948	Renken Master
1949–50	Milton Miller
1951–52	John F. Stay
1953–54	Carl Waller
1955–56	Louis M. Senger
1957–58	Thomas G. Brannen
1959–60	Patrick Neal Gallagher
1961–62	William H. Andrews
1963–64	Samuel Hyman
1965–66	John Chadwick
1967–68	Lee Jacobs
1969–70	Esther Greenberg
1971–72	Robert Bundy
1973–74	Louise M. Emond
1975	Abe Goodman
1976	Louise M. Emond

District Realigned

FIFTH DISTRICT COMMANDERS
PHILADELPHIA COUNTY

1919	James J. Lamond
1920	Thomas Moore
1921	I. G. Gordon Forster
1922	Dr. William E. Raken
1923–25	Thomas Moore
1926–27	Dr. William B. Pugh
1928–30	Robert J. Hanna
1931	Matthew Dombrowski
1932–33	William B. Clare
1934–35	John Pickard
1936–37	Joseph K. Schmid
1938–39	Owen Gerew
1940–41	Glenn Stefanowicz
1942–43	George Williams
1944–45	Clyde E. Rankin
1946–47	Ralph K. Weidner
1948–49	Thomas J. Fitzsimmons
1950–51	Joseph Ruczynski
1952–53	Stephen Berg
1954–55	Harry G. Fox, Jr.
1956–57	Frank Wenben
1958–59	Theodore F. Foedisch
1960–61	Stanley Lewandwoski
1962–63	Donald H. Jeffery
1964–65	Charles Gephart
1966–67	John J. King
1968–69	James Hartzell
1970–71	E. Paul Kunst
1972–73	George Winkler
1974–75	Joseph T. Schneider
1976–77	Leo A. Collins, Jr.
1978–79	Joseph W. Socha
1980–81	John E. Burroughs
1982–83	Robert Bartosh
1984–85	Edwin J. Smialkowski
1986–87	Edward M. Walczak
1988–89	James Benjamin
1989–91	Stanley Fabeszewski
1991–93	Fabian Marucci

SIXTH DISTRICT COMMANDERS
PHILADELPHIA COUNTY

1919	Leon Weinrott	William Muench
	William J. Smith	C. P. Franklin
	Clyde Mearkle	
1920	Thomas Moore	
1921	I. G. Gordon Forster	
1922	Dr. William E. Raken	
1923	John J. Owens	
1924–26	Dr. A. H. Wittmann	
1927–31	F. A. Kanter	
1932–35	Harry K. Stinger	
1936–37	Joseph I. Finnerty	
1939–40	Mark Villarose	
1941–42	Packey Long	
1943–44	Mahlon W. Smith	
1945–46	Thomas Brown	
1947–48	John P. Lavery	
1949–50	Harold R. Lacy	
1951–52	Francis J. Aitken	
1953–54	Thomas J. Kane	
1955–56	George J. Gardner	
1957–58	John J. O'Donnell	
1959	D. Leonard Rosenfeldt	
1960	D. Leonard Rosenfeldt / George Gardner	
1961–62	James J. Peck	
1963–64	Charles Polk	
1965–66	William V. Bobb, Jr.	
1967–68	John E. Boyce	
1969–70	George C. Baldauf	
1971–72	James R. Kelley	
1973–74	Joseph E. Sweeney	
1975–76	William Martin	
1977–78	James Lloyd	
1979–80	Albert J. Salmon	
1981–82	Joseph I. Abel	
1983–84	Glen Browell	
1985–86	Robert Boins	

1987–88	John McDevitt
1989–90	Eugene R. Smith
1990–92	Edmond F. Anderson
1992–93	Reynold C. Johnson

SEVENTH DISTRICT COMMANDERS
PHILADELPHIA COUNTY

1919	Millard D. Brown
	Charles H. Dearlove
1920	Thomas G. Moore
1921	I. G. Gordon Forster
1922	Dr. William E. Raken
1923–25	Samuel M. Lieberman
1926–27	Dr. W. R. Andress
1928	W. Whitney Ball/Charles I. Engard
1929	Charles I. Engard
1930–31	William H. Lukens
1932–33	Abe Kehr
1934–35	Norman Garrett
1936–37	Adam Goscinski
1938	William Birney
1939	Paul Foley
1940–41	William J. Green
1942–43	Martin B. McCann
1944–45	John J. Orr
1946–47	William Helriegel, Jr.
1948–49	George Roberts
1950–51	Stanley Root
1952–53	Matthew Brodzik
1954–55	Annette Eckman
1956–57	John F. Eckman
1958–59	Frank C. Kappler
1960–61	Paul A. Wolf
1962–63	Laurence J. DiStefano
1964–65	James Tyler
1966–67	E. Thomas Cammarota
1968–69	Joseph G. Mock, Jr.
1970–71	William J. Judge
1972–73	John H. Bowens
1974–75	Charles J. Tucker
1976–77	Charles W. Gossner
1978–79	Warren Keys
1980–81	Dominic J. Higgins, Jr.

1982	Kenneth Mickles
1983	John Jefferys
1984–85	George H. Carter
1986–87	Thomas J. Veney
1988–89	Harold Dewitt
1990–91	Richard Palmer
1992–93	Terry Lewis

EIGHTH DISTRICT COMMANDERS
CHESTER AND DELAWARE COUNTIES

1919	Richard Stevenson	Chester
	Ellis E. Stern	Coatesville
	John E. Johnson	West Chester
	Louis Apfelbaum	Coatesville
1920	Al Sproul, Jr.	Lansdowne
1921	Gilbert McIlvaine	Downingtown
1922–23	J. Norman Stephens	Lansdowne
1924–26	Dr. Carl Lofland	Kennett Square
1927	Robert W. Neall	Lansdowne
1928	Mervyn Turk	Chester
1929–30	L. Leroy Deninger	Phoenixville
1931	Langdon Cook	Lansdowne
1932	Lane Davis	Media
1933–34	Paul B. Dague	Downingtown
1935	William H. Whitaker	Upper Darby
1936	William H. Whitaker	Upper Darby
	John MacAlister	Glenolden
1937–38	Charles Malin	Malvern
1939–40	William Rhoades	Norwood
1941–42	Joseph Sheehan	Landenberg
1943	Howard E. McKay	Springfield
1944	Dixie D. Dryden	Chester
1945–46	Roy Walford	Parkesburg
1947–48	Charles J. Zenone	Upper Darby
1949–50	Thomas R. Plummer	Paoli
1951–52	Leo A. McDonald	Yeadon
1953–54	Harold Arnold	Kennett Square
1955–56	William Sweeney	Springfield
1957–58	Thomas W. O'Connor	Spring City
1959–60	Aloysius T. O'Donnell	Prospect Park
1961–62	C. Lewis Spare	Phoenixville
1963–64	Gerald P. Domenick	Wayne
1965–66	H. Richard Francis	Sharon Hill
1967	Ernest Jordan	West Chester
1967–68	Henry Sicoli	West Chester
1969–70	Frank K. Cheatley	Norwood

1971–72	Joseph Fletcher	Upper Darby
1973–74	F. Rodney Loper	West Chester
1975–76	Michael Janton	Aston
1977–78	Jules Falcone	Wayne
1979–80	Elwood Fahrenholtz	West Chester
1981–82	Emory W. Driscoll, Jr.	Aston
1983–84	Carmen R. Palladino	Prospect Park
1985–86	Raymond J. Sieben	Malvern
1987–88	James Gallagher	Newtown Square
1989–90	George H. Junkerman	Folsom
1991–92	Barry Amole	Spring City
1992–93	James F. Riley	Eddystone

NINTH DISTRICT COMMANDERS
BUCKS AND MONTGOMERY COUNTIES

1919	Eldred J. Pennell	Norristown
	Russell Reifsnyder	Pottstown
	Stanley H. Hunsicker	Norristown
	George VanBuskirk	Pottstown
	E. B. Krumbhaar	Flourtown
	E. E. Horner	Harriman
	T. F. Fitzgerald	Harriman
1920	George Ross	Doylestown
1921	W. Veryl Walton	Jenkintown
1922	Jacob C. Schmidt	Bristol
1923	Arthur T. Rush	Abington
1924–25	Jacob Miller	Hatboro
1926–29	Benjamin Howarth	Willow Grove
1930	William E. Zimmerman	Lansdale
1931–35	Leon Walt	Royersford
1936–37	Harold Reese	Ardmore
1938–39	Ray Hemmerly	Melrose Park
1940	Jacob Schmidt, Jr.	Bristol
1941	Paul Sine	Perkasie
1942–43	John C. Baxter	Philadelphia
1944–45	Clarence G. Brown	Jeffersonville
1946–47	Elmer Leddon	Willow Grove
1948–49	Herbert M. Walker	Langhorne
1950–51	Norman John	Pottstown
1952–53	Thomas M. Tressler, Jr.	Fort Washington
1954–55	Donald Knight	Roslyn
1956–57	Monroe Bethman	Doylestown
1958–59	Edward G. Wiley	Lansdale
1960–61	Adolph M. Lightman	Abington
1962–63	Harvey Gordon	Willow Grove
1964–65	Joseph V. Adams	Cheltenham
1966–67	Ernest W. Stiess	Langhorne
1968–69	H. Randall Rosenberger	
1970–71	Albert Hall, Jr.	Elkins Park
1972–73	Herman DeMatthews	Norristown
1974–75	Julius O. Kerper	Philadelphia

1976–77	Grover Kilmer	Doylestown
1978–79	E. Thomas Cammarota	North Wales
1980–81	Anthony R. Gallo	Washington
1982–83	Joseph A. Palermo	Ambler
1984–85	Harry V. Allen	Hatboro
1986–87	Joseph V. Glazier, Jr.	Quakertown
1988–89	Ivan R. Kerschner	Sellersville
1990–91	John E. Kelly	Ambler
1992–93	Irvine McGarvey	West Point

TENTH DISTRICT COMMANDERS
LANCASTER COUNTY

1919	Oliver J. Keller	Lancaster
1920	J. W. Wickersham	Lancaster
1921	John M. Groff	Lancaster
1922	K. L. Shirk	Lancaster
1923	H. R. Shreiner	Columbia
1924–26	Daniel B. Strickler	Lancaster
1927–28	Roy B. Sheetz	Mount Joy
1929–30	Hugh Eisemann	Ephrata
1931–32	Robert Waddell	Lancaster
1933–34	Gregg D. Breitegan	Columbia
1935–36	Wayne B. Ranck	New Holland
1937–38	Herbert Gansman	Lancaster
1939–40	Donald Bachman	Strassburg
1941–42	Daniel W. Shaub	Lancaster
1943–44	Milton H. Jacoby	Ephrata
1945–46	Henry C. Shank	Lancaster
1947–48	Ambrose S. Plummer	Elizabethtown
1949–50	Samuel B. Sheetz	East Petersburg
1951–52	Robert Herr	Quarryville
1953–54	Charles Mentzer	New Holland
1955–56	James Shaeffer	Mount Joy
1957–58	J. Paul Gerstenlauer	Ephrata
1959–60	Edgar O. Beck	New Holland
1961–62	Albert Lutz	Lititz
1963–64	Harry A. Raymond	Elizabethtown
1965–66	Harry S. Rapp	Lancaster
1967–68	Douglas Fitzwater	
1969–70	Jerry U. Davis	
1971–72	William C. Hartsough	Lancaster
1973–74	Howard W. Stouffer	Lancaster
1975–76	Phares M. Ecenrode	Ephrata
1977–78	John Specht	New Holland
1979–80	Earl B. Rettew	Landisville
1981–82	Robert R. Forbes	Lancaster
1983–84	Gerald R. Schuldt	Elizabethtown
1985–86	William C. Hartsough	Willow Street

1987–88	Richard J. Appler, Jr.	Mount Joy
1989–90	L. Quintin Eisemann	Ephrata
1991–92	David D. Todd	Lancaster
1992–93	James Heisey	Lancaster

ELEVENTH DISTRICT COMMANDERS
LACKAWANNA COUNTY

1919	None	
1920	R. B. McLau	Scranton
1921	R. B. McClave	Scranton
1922	Dr. Leo P. Gibbons	Scranton
1923	Frank Moran	Scranton
1924–25	J. Harry Morosini	Scranton
1926–27	Richard Walsh	Scranton
1928–29	Michael Onze	Olyphant
1930–31	William C. Fauver	Scranton
1932–33	John B. McDade	Taylor
1934	John Harrison	Archbald
1935	Walter Kohler	Old Forge
1936–37	Joseph Rosar	Scranton
1938–39	B. J. O'Hara	Scranton
1940–41	Roy Jones	Scranton
1942–43	Frank X. Murray	Scranton
1944–45	Paul Ord	Scranton
1946–47	George J. Lopata	Jermyn
1948–49	James A. Reap	Archbald
1950–51	Fred Berry	Scranton
1952–53	Joseph Graham	Scranton
1954–55	Dr. Almo J. Sebastianelli	Jessup
1956–57	Thomas Priblo	Olyphant
1957	William T. Malone	Scranton
1958–59	Thomas J. Evans	Scranton
1960–61	William Kays	Dunmore
1962–63	Chester P. Tracewski	Eynon
1964–65	Patrick J. Wastella	Old Forge
1966–67	John J. Dunn, Sr.	Scranton
1968–69	Edmund Bojnowski	
1970–71	Prosper Spalletta	Dunmore
1972–73	Charles Strouse	Moscow
1974–75	Stanley Golden	Dunmore
1976	James Byrne	Olyphant
1977	Andre C. Major	Gouldsboro
1978–79	Robert Reilly	Scranton

1980–81	Andrew Major, Jr.	Gouldsboro
1982	Robert E. Reilly	Scranton
1983	Frank J. Zeranski	Moscow
1984–85	Arlington Phillips	Scranton
1986–87	Mark D. Evans	Carbondale
1988–89	Frank Matyjevich	Dunmore
1990–91	Carl Weber	Dickson City
1992–93	Michael Hynak	Jessup

TWELFTH DISTRICT COMMANDERS
LUZERNE COUNTY

1919	W. F. Dobson	Wilkes-Barre
	George A. Patterson	Hazelton
	Ed Brown	Wilkes-Barre
	Byron Wear	Hazelton
1920–21	Dr. F. B. Archer	Wilkes-Barre
1922	Frank L. Pinola	Wilkes-Barre
1923	E. F. McGovern	Wilkes-Barre
1924–26	Robert R. Oberender	Freeland
1927–28	Louis N. Edwards	Nanticoke
1929	Leonard Morgan	Forty-Fort
1930	Joseph Schneider	Wilkes-Barre
1931	Dr. John Lavin	Swoyersville
1932	Joseph Keller	Wilkes-Barre
1933–34	J. M. Sloan	Hazelton
1935–36	Charles Cook	West Pittston
1937–38	Robert Miller	Kingston
1939	Leo Castle	Kingston
1939–40	Fred Bachman	Hazelton
1941–42	Michael M. Markowitz	Swoyersville
1943	Dr. Elmer T. Williams	Plymouth
1944	Frank A. Goeckl	Plymouth
1945–46	James McCrackin	Kingston
1947–48	Oscar Renfer	Pittston
1949–50	Paul Selecky	Wilkes-Barre
1951–52	Herman Shepard	Wilkes-Barre
1953–54	Leonard Stigora	Nanticoke
1955–56	Fred J. Shupnik	Luzerne
1957–58	Louis J. Greco	West Wyoming
1959–60	John R. Gallagher	Freeland
1961–62	Nello S. Carozzoni	Wilkes-Barre
1963–64	Michell Czoch	Wilkes-Barre
1965–66	Peter Baller	Plains
1967–68	William J. Horan	Plains
1969–70	Joseph J. Chevitski	
1971–72	Walter E. Condon	Swoyersville
1973–74	Edward McGeehan	Hazelton

1975–76	Russell Dugan	Kingston
1977–78	Benjamin Zabriski	Plains
1979–80	Albert E. Prebola	Wilkes-Barre
1981–82	George Hufford	Kingston
1983–84	Edwin Markiewicz	Nanticoke
1985–86	John D. Joseph	Wilkes-Barre
1987–88	Edward T. Sobolewski	Wilkes-Barre
1989–90	David G. Evans	West Pittston
1991–92	Bill S. Hoag	Avoca
1992–93	Bryan Obert	Plymouth

THIRTEENTH DISTRICT COMMANDERS
SCHUYLKILL COUNTY

1919	Clinton A. Shaefer	Pottsville
	Thomas A. Rehr	Pottsville
	Stanley Davis	Pottsville
	Seth T. Reese	Pottsville
1920	Paul Houck	Shenandoah
1921	J. E. Schlottman	Pottsville
1922	Dr. Robert W. Lenker	Schuylkill Haven
1923–27	Charles A. Gebert	Tamaqua
1928–29	William G. Morris	St. Clair
1930–33	Walter Evans	Mahanoy City
1934–35	James M. Donohue	Coaldale
1936–37	David Baird	Pottsville
1938–39	Edward Burmeister	Ashland
1940–41	Homer D. Sarge	Pine Grove
1942–43	Harry F. Koenig	Pottsville
1944–45	Martin V. McGuire	Shenandoah
1946–47	William Boussum	Cressona
1948–49	Lewis McKrebs	Port Carbon
1950–51	Joseph Halka	Mahanoy City
1952–53	George Martz	Shenandoah
1954–55	Paul Walters	Pine Grove
1956–57	Richard Bassler	Tamaqua
1958–59	Daniel Kimmel	Tower City
1960–61	Joseph J. O'Toole, Jr.	Port Carbon
1962–63	Robert F. Ertwine	Ringtown
1964–65	Charles A. Bubeck	Schuylkill Haven
1966–67	Charles L. Marquardt	Girardville
1968–69	Joseph F. Kline	Tamaqua
1970–71	John A. Zulick	Schuylkill Haven
1972–73	Kenneth Miller	Pine Grove
1974–75	Henry Pangrazzi	Sheppton
1976–77	John M. Domin	Coaldale
1978–79	Joseph M. Boyle	McAdoo
1980–81	James E. Manion	St. Clair
1982–83	Warren G. Williams	Elizabethville
1984–85	James Arner	Coaldale

1986–87	John Kukta	Minersville
1988–89	William L. Paul	Morea
1990–91	William E. Evans	Tamaqua
1992–93	Eugene W. Strine	Williamstown

FOURTEENTH DISTRICT COMMANDERS
BERKS AND LEHIGH COUNTIES

1919	Harry C. Blank	Allentown
	Dallas Gangewer	Allentown
	George A. Rick	Reading
	Guy K. Sembower	Reading
1920	Ralph M. Kendall	Reading
1921	Edward H. Quinn	Allentown
1922	Earl L. Weaver	Allentown
1923	Samuel Rothermel	Fleetwood
1924–28	Clarence R. Nagle	Allentown
1929–32	Morris Schifreen	Catasauqua
1933–34	Milton Harris	Reading
1935–36	Frank E. Gwynn	Allentown
1937	Clarence P. Gring	Douglasville
1938	Charles R. McCann	Reading
1939–40	Nick Morrell	Bethlehem
1941–42	Jesse R. Conner	West Reading
1943–44	Fred W. Fleischman	Allentown
1945–46	Morgan D. Reinbold	Reading
1947–48	Robert W. Hausman	Allentown
1949–50	Elmer B. Miller	Strausstown
1951–52	Frederick H. E. Dorney	Allentown
1953–54	Arthur Y. Miller	Boyertown
1955–56	George F. Bruno	Bethlehem
1957–58	John L. Harr	Reading
1959–60	Ernest Kehm	Allentown
1961–62	Ralph C. Witman	Bernville
1963–64	Norman D. Fenner	Fullerton
1965–66	Samuel W. Bolton	Hamburg
1967–68	Fred J. Pellegrino	Coplay
1969–70	Linford Breuninger	
1971–72	Luther J. Minnich	Slatington
1973–74	Norman J. Greeland	Reading
1975–76	John Zweisdak	Allentown
1977–78	William H. Seifert	Birdsboro
1979–80	Stanley W. Reinhard, Jr.	Coplay
1981–82	James Jackson	Reading

1983–84	Dennis Casciano	Bethlehem
1985–86	Donald J. Razmyslowski	Boyertown
1987–88	Paul Getz	Bethlehem
1989–90	Alonzo Price	Reading
1991–92	Melvin T. Deisenroth	Allentown
1992–93	Lothair E. Dreibelbis	Fleetwood

FIFTEENTH DISTRICT COMMANDERS
BRADFORD, PIKE, SUSQUEHANNA, WAYNE, AND WYOMING COUNTIES

1919	Leslie J. Perry	Powell
	Joseph W. Beaman	Towanda
	Ed D. Katz	Honesdale
1920–21	Joseph W. Beaman	Towanda
1922	Joseph Walsh	Honesdale
1923–25	Joseph W. Beaman	Towanda
1926–27	Charles R. Schweizer	Honesdale
1928–31	Lester Albert	Susquehanna
1932–35	George Murphy	Hawley
1936–37	James Murray	Forrest City
1938–39	Walter W. White	Snederkerville
1940–41	Almon D. Baker	Tunkhannock
1942–43	John P. Kokolias	Matamorus
1944–45	Charles Millar	Hawley
1946–47	Hilbert M. Melhuish	Montrose
1948–49	Randolph Grace	Towanda
1950–51	Richard Ayer	Tunkhannock
1952–53	William T. McGinniss	Honesdale
1954	John M. Doney	Susquehanna
1954–55	Fred B. Fancher	Brackney
1956–57	George Miller	Wyalusing
1958–59	Harold E. Davis	Factoryville
1960–61	Gerald A. Blitz	Milford
1962–63	I. Reines Skier	Hawley
1964–65	Daniel C. Deobold, Sr.	Brackney
1966–67	Joseph H. Baker	Wyalusing
1968–69	Boris Saranchuk	
1970–71	Esther Birney	Sayre
1972–73	Stuart W. MacNeal	Montrose
1974–75	John Sheleman	Dushore
1976–77	Albert Remsnyder	Towanda
1978–79	Ernest F. George	East Stroudsburg
1980–81	Peter Amirault	Susquehanna
1982–83	George A. Dutcher, Jr.	Hallstead
1984–85	Carl Platner	Susquehanna

1986	David Rewiski	Lake Como
1986–87	Richard J. Ayers	Meshoppen
1988–89	Arnold W. Vealey	Matamorus
1989	Richard J. Ayers	Meshoppen
1990–91	George B. Dutcher, Jr.	Hallstead
1992–93	Michael DiNapoli	Matamoras

SIXTEENTH DISTRICT COMMANDERS
CLINTON, LYCOMING, POTTER, AND TIOGA COUNTIES

1919	Bynon C. Houck	Williamsport
	W. Boyd Kline	Williamsport
	L. S. Spangle	Williamsport
	Francis S. Bodine	Wellsboro
	George H. Norman	Arnot
1920	Lyle Spangle	Williamsport
1921	Edgar Sones	Williamsport
1922	Edward Russell	Mansfield
1923	Carl O. Hoover	Lock Haven
1924–26	L. A. Henderson	Montgomery
1927–28	H. R. Bowman	Williamsport
1929–32	H. G. Strait	Mansfield
1933–34	William J. Molenkopf	Williamsport
1935–36	Mark L. Tingsley	Blossburg
1937–38	F. E. McIntyre	Lock Haven
1939	Fred Bush	South Williamsport
1940	William Murray	Jersey Shore
1941–42	Dr. Ross H. Jones	Coudersport
1943–44	Albert C. Nichols	Lock Haven
1945–46	Freeman F. Hall	Williamsport
1947–48	Emory Rockwell	Wellsboro
1949–50	R. O. Raymond	Renovo
1951–52	Owen A. Johnson	Jersey Shore
1953–54	Kenneth Brace	Mansfield
1955–56	Carl Vroman	Renovo
1957–58	Thomas H. Harris	Williamsport
1959–60	Hugh B. Cunningham	Blossburg
1961–62	Edwin D. Tyndale	Lock Haven
1963–64	Walter Carroll	Muncy
1965	Charles W. Norwood	Ulysses
1966	William Schroeder	Coudersport
1967–68	Hugh Cunningham	Blossburg
1969–70	Forrest A. Yost	
1971–72	Richard W. Snyder	Williamsport
1973–74	Joseph Zelinski, Jr.	Coudersport
1975–76	John Cashner	Avis

1977–78	Andrew Condo	Williamsport
1979–80	John W. Seyler, Jr.	Loganton
1981–82	Clifford O'Neal	Montoursville
1983	John W. Wolford	Blanchard
1983–84	James W. Workman, Sr.	Castanea
1984	Forest E. Hafer, Jr.	Williamsport
1985–86	Bradley H. Oechler	Williamsport
1987–88	Frank H. Winkelman	North Bend
1989–90	E. Robert Niven	Hughesville
1991–92	William Lincoln	Genesee
1992–93	Philip H. Proctor	Renovo

SEVENTEENTH DISTRICT COMMANDERS
COLUMBIA, MONTOUR, NORTHUMBERLAND, AND SULLIVAN COUNTIES

1919	Carl Hecht	Milton
	C. K. Morganroth	Shamokin
	Thomas F. Steele	Shamokin
	Frank H. Herbine	Berwick
	Frank L. Distlehurst	Berwick
1920	Dr. L. A. Cobbett	Milton
1921	Jesse M. Kline	Shamokin
1922	Abe Gennaria	Bloomsburg
1923–29	Joseph Fox	Milton
1930–31	Al Landis	Mount Carmel
1932–33	William J. Klein	Northumberland
1934–35	Ray Howells	Mount Carmel
1936–37	Daniel R. McKinney	Sunbury
1938–39	A. C. Morgan	Berwick
1940–41	Donald J. Zimmerman	Shamokin
1942–43	Dr. R. Y. Grone	Danville
1944–45	Milton D. Moore	Sunbury
1946–47	Stanley Fuhrer	Dalmatia
1948–49	Warren C. Roseman	Shamokin
1950–51	Andrew T. Murray	Sunbury
1952–53	Joseph P. Gavenonis	Mildred
1954–55	Dr. Robert E. Allen	Mount Carmel
1956–57	A. L. Wintersteen	Danville
1958–59	Chester Duchman	Montandon
1960–61	Harry V. Klein, Jr	Sunbury
1962–63	Sanford S. Marateck	Shamokin
1964–65	William D. Packer	Sunbury
1966–67	Lee C. Shaffer	Sunbury
1968–69	Richard Krebs	Milton
1970–71	Robert S. Bastian	Milton
1972–73	John S. Wondoloski	Centralia
1974–75	Sam Morris	Bloomsburg
1976–77	Robert W. Joe	New Columbia
1978–79	Joseph L. Whapham	Danville
1980–81	Donald V. Thomas	Bloomsburg
1982–83	Daniel C. Swank	Northumberland

1984–85	David A. Packer	Sunbury
1986–87	Dale A. Herritt	Bloomsburg
1988–89	Ross V. Fegley	Lewisburg
1990–91	Robert C. Wright	Bloomsburg
1992–93	William R. Neitz	Sunbury

EIGHTEENTH DISTRICT COMMANDERS
HUNTINGDON, JUNIATA, MIFFLIN, PERRY, SNYDER, AND UNION COUNTIES

1919	A. M. Aurand, Jr.	Beaver Springs
	Miller A. Johnson	Lewisburg
	Joseph Snyder	Lewisburg
	George S. Denithorne	Huntingdon
1920–21	A. M. Aurand, Jr.	Beaver Springs
1922	Rev. George J. College	Huntingdon
1923	Dr. E. J. Williams	Huntingdon
1924–25	Frank W. Kurtz	Huntingdon
1926–28	S. B. Wolfe	Lewisburg
1929–32	George H. Ervin	Waynesboro
1933–34	John Y. Wills	Duncannon
1935–38	D. Walker Woods	Lewistown
1939	Louis Harris	Lewisburg
1940–41	Carl Rosebrock	Lewistown
1942–44	William D. Hetherington	Selinsgrove
1945–46	Harry Zeiders	Newport
1947–48	Marshall Awkerman	Mount Union
1949–50	Samuel Rapp	Mifflintown
1951–52	Edward Oser	Huntingdon
1953–54	Kenneth Swartzel	Lewistown
1955–56	J. LeRoy Cumbler	Newport
1957–58	Clyde Hockenberry	McVeytown
1959–60	Warren E. Figard	Rock Hill Furnace
1961–62	Kenneth L. Shively	Mifflinburg
1963–64	Rudolph R. Wagner	McClure
1965–66	George E. Wetzel, Jr.	New Berlin
1967–68	Thomas Allander	Duncannon
1969–70	Chester S. Peterson	
1971–72	William Wills	Harrisburg
1973	James E. Casselberry	
1974	Orville Snare	Huntingdon
1975–76	Elmer L. Hafer	Lewisburg
1977–78	Norwood Deibler	Duncannon
1979–80	Ernest Renninger	Selinsgrove
1981–82	Jeffrey L. Seler	McClure

1983–84	Harold E. Goodling	Newport
1985–86	Harry J. Miller	New Berlin
1987–88	Lionel Blyler	Millmont
1989–90	Nathaniel Trice	Mount Union
1991–92	Ralph E. Wolfe	Newport
1992–93	John Hafer	Mifflinburg

NINETEENTH DISTRICT COMMANDERS
CUMBERLAND, DAUPHIN, AND LEBANON COUNTIES

1919	Garfield J. Phillips	Harrisburg
	Mark T. Milnor	Harrisburg
	E. S. Stackpole	Harrisburg
	Paul Gilbert	Harrisburg
1920	Mark Milnor	Harrisburg
1921	Patrick Sweeney	Harrisburg
1922	Dr. John E. Marshall	Lebanon
1923	George C. Neff	Harrisburg
1924–25	Coleman B. Mark	Harrisburg
1926–27	John I. Carroll	Carlisle
1928–29	Paul Yoder	Palmyra
1930–31	J. Russell Sheffer	Middletown
1932–33	Hobart Hopkins	New Cumberland
1934–35	Norman Streicher	Annville
1936–37	Abe Shelley	Steelton
1938–39	John E. Martin	Camp Hill
1940–41	Harry K. Fishman	Lebanon
1942–43	Earl A. Peters	Harrisburg
1944–45	Robert W. Fish	Mechanicsburg
1946–47	John L. Louser	Lebanon
1948–49	Joseph Huss	Hummelstown
1950–51	W. Mac Pittinger	Carlisle
1952–53	J. Ben Dubson	Harrisburg
1954	Howard Goodman	Harrisburg
1955	Ray E. Taylor	Harrisburg
1956–57	Dorrance Peckens	New Cumberland
1958–59	Robert B. Shaeffer	Myerstown
1960–61	Raymond K. Weaver	Middletown
1962–63	Bernard Steiner	Mechanicsburg
1964–65	John E. Gilbert	Fredericksburg
1966–67	Eugene Buggy	Lykens
1968–69	Richard Hanlen	
1970–71	Ernest P. Zserai	Jonestown
1972–73	John Q. Waters	Harrisburg
1974–75	Thomas A. Payne	Chambersburg
1976–77	Harvey R. Kegerreis	Richland

1978–79	Dominic D. DiFrancesco	Middletown
1980–81	Jesse Startzel, Jr.	Camp Hill
1982–83	Leonard Gerhart	Fredericksburg
1984–85	Fred Wagner	Hummelstown
1986–87	Jay A. Weaver	Newville
1988–89	Richard Y. Roof	Lebanon
1990–91	John Kuhn	Middletown
1992–93	George Reeder	Mechanicsburg

TWENTIETH DISTRICT COMMANDERS
CAMBRIA COUNTY

1919	Andrew F. Fisher	Johnstown
	C. A. Buettner	Johnstown
	Charles Kress	Johnstown
1920	Dr. R. J. Sagerson	Johnstown
1921	Dr. J. B. Nason	Tyrone
1922–23	Dr. R. J. Sagerson	Johnstown
1924–25	Dr. Dan P. Ray	Johnstown
1926–29	George Foster	Johnstown
1930	Walter Kress	Johnstown
1930–32	Thomas Bender	Lilly
1933	Carl C. Tinstman	Johnstown
1934	Max Bloomberg	Johnstown
1935–38	Curtis Paessler	Johnstown
1939–40	Edwin F. Green	Portage
1945–46	Herman C. Riblett	Johnstown
1947–48	Fred Morley	Barnesboro
1949–50	Joseph (James) Bernard	Gallitzin
1951–52	Samuel Brooks	Johnstown
1953	Paul J. Wills	Loretta
1953–54	William Stein	Cresson
1955–56	Paul R. Jones	Ebensburg
1957–58	Jesse W. Cogley	Patton
1959–60	Anslem Julian	Gallitzin
1961–62	Ronald A. Daugherty	Johnstown
1963–64	Elmer J. Shenk	Cresson
1965–66	John R. Makdad	Johnstown
1967–68	Harry S. Keith	Ebensburg
1969–70	John J. Toskey	
1971–72	R. Raymond Lenz	Cresson
1973–74	Edward L. Diveley, Jr.	Johnstown
1975–76	Don Stoy	Ebensburg
1977–78	Howard A. Burkhart	Gallitzin
1979–80	Cletus E. Noon	Johnstown
1981–82	Charles L. Penatzer	Johnstown
1983–84	Donald W. Wilson	Portage
1987	James E. McQuown, Jr.	Johnstown

1987–88	Francis Van Blargan	Lilly
1989–90	Donald W. Wilson	Portage
1991–92	Clarence Helsel	Portage
1992–93	Thomas Kroskey	Gallitzin

TWENTY-FIRST DISTRICT COMMANDERS
BEDFORD AND BLAIR COUNTIES

1919	James S. Richards	Altoona
	Webster C. Calvin	Altoona
1920	Dr. R. J. Sagerson	Johnstown
1921	Dr. J. B. Nason	Tyrone
1922	Paul R. Kuhn	Altoona
1923	Dr. Walter E. Lotz	Tyrone
1924–25	George D. Wands	Tyrone
1926–27	George L. Horner	Roaring Springs
1928–29	Jay M. Walker	Everett
1930–31	Floyd Hoenstine	Hollidaysburg
1932–33	Robert Amos	Bedford
1934–35	E. S. Warner	Hollidaysburg
1936–37	Ivan White	Saxton
1937	Dr. John Galbraith	Altoona
1938–39	C. Wilbur Van Scoyoc	Tyrone
1940–41	George C. Heit	Bedford
1942–43	Warren C. McCarty	Claysburg
1944	Dr. Ralph A. Howard	Everett
1945	Jason Eshelman	Everett
1946–47	Lee E. Wertz	Tyrone
1948–49	William M. Gearinger	Six Mile Run
1950–51	L. W. F. Haberstroh	Altoona
1952–53	J. Chester Foor	Bedford
1954–55	James Truitt	Bellwood
1956–57	Robert Hoenstine	Claysburg
1958–59	A. John Garritano	Altoona
1960–61	J. Merle Closson	Roaring Springs
1962	Clyde M. Querry	Altoona
1963	John G. Gibboney *(Honorary)*	Tyrone
1964–65	George F. Yeager *(Honorary)*	Altoona
1966–67	Reginald W. Greaser	Bedford
1968–69	R. King Bowser	
1970–71	Victor T. Raia	Altoona
1972–73	James Kilmartin	Tyrone
1974–75	Arthur T. Colyer	Tyrone

1976–77	William F. Keagy	Martinsburg
1978–79	Paul Shaefer	Tyrone
1980–81	Daniel Fanelli	Altoona
1982–83	Willis F. Irvin	Tyrone
1984–85	Harry F. Carney	New Paris
1986–87	Arthur Jock, Sr.	Bellwood
1988–89	Frank Shaffer	Six Mile Run
1990–91	Walter S. Edwards	Williamsburg
1992	Harry F. Carney	New Paris
1993	Walter S. Edwards	Williamsburg

TWENTY-SECOND DISTRICT COMMANDERS
ADAMS, FRANKLIN, FULTON, AND YORK COUNTIES

1919	Ray O. Dunkle	Chambersburg
	Crawford D. McLay	Chambersburg
	John W. Hartman	Gettysburg
1920	William H. Kurtz	York
1921	John C. Hoffman	York
1922	Richard Y. Naill	Hanover
1923	Paul E. Zeigler	York
1924–26	Robert M. Laird	Hanover
1927–28	A. S. Benedict	Dallastown
1929–32	Charles R. Lose	York
1933–34	Herbert C. Hoover	Glen Rock
1935–36	Wilbur Brown	Waynesboro
1937–38	Samuel Serff	Hanover
1939–40	Myron Bowers	Chambersburg
1941–42	James W. Hefferman	York
1943–44	Stanton D. House	Aspers
1945–46	Jerry G. Allen	Scotland
1947–48	Herbert Smith	Red Lion
1949–50	Wilbur Geiselman	Gettysburg
1951–52	Walter S. Metz	Chambersburg
1953–54	Earl Sollenberger	York
1955–56	Paul Fox	Gettysburg
1957–58	George Klee	St. Thomas
1959–60	M. Russell Hamme	Dover
1961–62	O. Perry House	Aspers
1963–64	Charles C. Harrison	St. Thomas
1965–66	Carroll J. Noel	Hanover
1967–68	Harry Reed	Waynesboro
1969–70	Gerald B. Flinchbaugh	
1971–72	Eugene C. Eichelberger	St. Thomas
1973–74	James K. Beaverson	New Cumberland
1975–76	Jasper Stouffer, Jr.	Chambersburg
1977–78	Dale A. Sprenkle	Dallastown
1979–80	Lynn S. Bard	McConnellsburg
1981–82	Leon Jenkins	York
1983–84	Paul Nunemaker	Chambersburg

1985–86	Kathryn H. Welsh	York
1987–88	Robert W. Kelley	Fayetteville
1989	James R. Reaver	Aspers
1989–90	Robert E. Guise	Gardners
1991–92	Lester F. Kipe, Jr.	Waynesboro
1992–93	Robert Miller, Jr.	Dover

TWENTY-THIRD DISTRICT COMMANDERS
CAMERON, CENTRE, CLEARFIELD, AND MCKEAN COUNTIES

1919	Guy H. Lawhead	Clearfield
	Warren Jones	Clearfield
	Paul M. Gnetzel	Bellefonte
1920	Fred P. Schoomaker	Bradford
1921	J. J. Pentz	DuBois
1922	J. M. Chase	Clearfield
1923–26	A. W. Sheasley	Emporium
1927	James H. Reppert	Phillipsburg
	M. E. Meese	Phillipsburg
1928–29	M. E. Meese	Phillipsburg
1930–31	Bernal Connelly	Ludlow
1932–34	T. Reilly Lytle	Clearfield
1935	Charles Freeman	Phillipsburg
1936037	T. Reilly Lytle	Clearfield
1938–39	William Reese	Port Allegheny
1940–41	William McMullin	Millheim
1942	Dr. Hugh J. Ryan	Bedford
1943	Leonard Reck	Bradford
1944–45	Samuel D. Rinesmith	Bellefonte
1946–47	Rome L. Lunn	Emporium
1948–49	Robert M. Hershey	Clearfield
1950–51	Robert C. Denning	Bradford
1952–53	Paul Beardslee	Bellefonte
1954–55	Leo Dolan	Mount Jewett
1956–57	Ben Finger	DuBois
1958–59	Lloyd Mulvihill	Crosby
1960	Meredith M. Coldren	State College
1961	Thomas J. O'Hargan	Bradford
1962–63	John C. Mann	Clearfield
1964–65	Frank Berman	Emporium
1966–67	A. Hal Reede	State College
1968–69	Harold J. Witchen	
1970–71	L. James Milliron	Clearfield
1972–73	Elwin H. Irwin	Eldred
1974–75	Meredith M. Coldren	State College
1976–77	Albert E. Mische	Centre Hall

1978–79	Howard F. McCollough	Smethport
1980–81	Elmer D. Kessling	Port Matilda
1982–83	Robert Yeager	DuBois
1984–85	Willard Babcock	Smethport
1986–87	John J. King	DuBois
1988–89	Donald J. Anspauch	Bellefonte
1990–91	Kenneth D. Royer	Spring Mills
1992–93	Richard A. Coccimiglio	Penfield

TWENTY-FOURTH DISTRICT COMMANDERS
FAYETTE AND SOMERSET COUNTIES

1919	Alfred Pearson, Jr.	Somerset
	M. G. McCrum	Somerset
	Michael J. Hudock	Uniontown
1920–21	Dr. S. A. Baltz	Uniontown
1922	B. C. Jones	Connellsville
1923	Correll J. Poole	Connellsville
1924–30	Carl C. Tinstman	Uniontown
1931	Paul H. Griffith	Uniontown
1932–34	Carl Hoffman	Somerset
1935–36	Alex Carlier	Port Marion
1937–38	Oscar Sutliffe	Somerset
1939–40	Francis Brady	Connellsville
1941–42	William E. Griffith	Somerset
1943–44	Wilbur E. Wilson	Brownsville
1945–46	Merle Beam	Windber
1947–48	Hugh W. Flenniken	Uniontown
1949–50	M. F. Beamer	Meyersdale
1951–52	John W. Collins	Connellsville
1953–54	Edward Herring	Somerset
1955–56	Julius Gaggiani	Republic
1957–58	George Sheavly	Berlin
1959–60	Robert D. Warman	Uniontown
1961–62	E. A. Morin	Somerset
1963–64	William A. Chrise	Fairchance
1965–66	Robert F. Bittner	Meyersdale
1967–68	Frank H. Parry	Charleroi
1969–70	Edward J. Drwal	
1971–72	Frank H. Parry	Charleroi
1973–74	Francis W. Maust	Berlin
1975–76	Humphrey J. Lukachik	Uniontown
1977–78	John Steinkirchner	Somerset
1979–80	Mario Antonucci	Hiller
1981–82	Michael Knapp	Windber
1983–84	John P. Moores, Jr.	Brownsville
1985–86	Karl R. Landis	Somerset
1987–88	Frank H. Parry	Charleroi

1988–89	Donald L. Baker	Rockwood
1991–92	Ronald Lape	Hiller
1992–93	Gerald L. Zorn	Rockwood

TWENTY-FIFTH DISTRICT COMMANDERS
GREENE AND WASHINGTON COUNTIES

1919	Alex W. Johns	Monessen
	Jay Garman	Monessen
1920	L. McK. Crumrine	Washington
1921	Dr. J. H. Frew	New Brighton
1922–25	L. McK. Crumrine	Washington
1926–28	Guy Woodward	Washington
1929–31	John Curran	Washington
1932–33	J. Ernest Isherwood	Waynesburg
1934–36	William B. Dinsmore	Washington
1937–38	Dr. H. H. McBurney	Avella
1939–41	Louis Nagy	Monongahela
1942–43	William J. Long	Washington
1944–45	John Stoup	Waynesburg
1946–47	Abe Ruben	Donora
1948–49	John T. Schwartz	Charleroi
1950–51	Herman Hartman	Washington
1952–53	James J. Reardon	Millsboro
1954–55	August Sismondo	Charleroi
1956–57	James Sykes	Pittsburgh
1958–59	Joseph I. Harshman	Fredericktown
1960–61	John Titus	Jefferson
1962–63	David Lonich	Fredericktown
1964–65	Michael P. Cvetan	Crucible
1966–67	Clinton W. Wright	Houston
1968–69	Charles W. Meadows	
1970–71	Wesley Wayne Philp	Fredericktown
1972–73	Floyd Haney	Mather
1974–75	Raymond H. Smith	McDonald
1976–77	Robert Lusk	Finleyville
1978–79	Carl Spaziani	Monongahela
1980–81	Walter Pasierbek	Washington
1982–83	Peter Devecka	Fredericktown
1983	Walter Pasierbek	Washington
1984–85	Gregory G. Amoroso	Monongahela
1986–87	Charles G. Pollacci	Charleroi
1988–89	Gasper J. Impiccini	Clarksville
1990–91	Donald R. Shipley	Roscoe
1992–93	August Cerini	Donora

TWENTY-SIXTH DISTRICT COMMANDERS
BEAVER, BUTLER, AND LAWRENCE COUNTIES

1919	Meyer Berkman	Beaver Falls
	Brainard Matheny	Beaver Falls
	Eugene Hoops	Beaver
	Stuart Gray	Butler
1920	L. McK. Crumrine	Washington
1921–22	Dr. J. H. Frew	New Brighton
1923–26	F. A. Weber	Beaver Falls
1927–28	Patrick Dempsey	New Castle
1929–30	Mike J. Kane	Aliquippa
1931–32	Charles Edwards	Rochester
1933–34	Clair Ross	Butler
1935–36	E. H. Markey	Monaca
	Frank D. Moulter	
1937–38	Guy Wadlinger	New Castle
1939–40	Dennis E. Caine	Ellwood City
1941–42	James H. Collins	Cabot
1943–44	William L. Mitsch	New Brighton
1945–46	A. Lewis Conn	New Castle
1947–48	Paul R. Faux	Butler
1949–50	Joseph Bontempo	Aliquippa
1951–52	R. Wayne Baird	Ellwood City
1953–54	Robert Crawford	Butler
1955–56	James Pfeifer	Rochester
1957–58	Kenneth E. Freed	Wampum
1959–60	Tony Rico	Harrisville
1961–62	George D. Yorns	Beaver
1963–64	James Gabriel	New Castle
1965–66	Chester W. Marburger	Mars
1967–68	Dom Presto	Baden
1969–70	Ray Matthews	
1971–72	Peter J. Standish	Mars
1973–74	Stephen U. Crano	Midland
1975–76	Earl Hildebrand	New Castle
1977–78	Lillian L. Sloan	Butler
1979–80	Charles A. Campbell, Jr.	Baden
1981–82	George W. Curry	New Castle

1983–84	Arthur C. Hollerman	Zelienople
1985–86	James Ellis	Rochester
1987–88	Carl R. Forkey	New Castle
1989–90	Edward M. Heeter	Petrolia
1991–92	Lewis Shaeffer	Rochester
1992–93	James Hales	New Alexandria

TWENTY-SEVENTH DISTRICT COMMANDERS
ARMSTRONG, CLARION, INDIANA, AND JEFFERSON COUNTIES

1919	Norman N. Duncan	Indiana
	Charles J. McClain	Indiana
1920	J. Frank Graff	Kittanning
1921	C. C. McClain	Indiana
1922–25	Dr. C. A. Rogers	Freeport
1926–33	D. C. McCallum	Leechburg
1934–35	William F. Smith	Punxsutawney
1936	Dr. Walter Dick	Brookville
1937	Leonard McQuown	Punxsutawney
1938	Roy E. Penfield	Indiana
1939	W. Carl Miller	Ford City
1940–41	J. H. McClaine	East Brady
1942	M. R. Tibby	Punxsutawney
1943	Clinton M. File	Indiana
1944	George L. Ralston	Freeport
1945	C. B. Long	Clarion
1946	Jackson R. Dodson	Punxsutawney
1947	Lawrence Redding	Indiana
1948	John J. Hobaugh	Ford City
1949	Harold L. Bowman	New Bethlehem
1950	Carl L. Brocius	Reynoldsville
1951	Clinton Myers	Indiana
1952	Louis Goldman	Ford City
1953	Eugene L. Klinger	St. Petersburg
1954	Francis E. Wehrle	Punxsutawney
1955	Kenneth Davis	Homer City
1956	R. Franklin Matthews	Parker
1957	Thomas W. Hosack	Clarion
1958	Adam Nava	Brockway
1959	Kenneth Davis	Homer City
1960	Thomas Scott	Kittanning
1961	Eugene Thompson	Foxburg
1962	Ernest Cavazza	Punxsutawney
1963	John C. Smith	Indiana
1964	Audley D. Kinter	Apollo
1965	Robert S. Thompson	Shippenville

1966	Francis E. Wehrle	Punxsutawney
1967	Kenneth Davis	Homer City
1968	Edward Walbert	
1969	Donald Baker	
1970	Gerald W. Hice	
1971	John Gearhart	Cherry Tree
1972	Donald E. Murrin	Petrolia
1973	William Kinter	Clarion
1974	Earl W. Corbett	Summerville
1975	Michael Machulsky	Saltsburg
1976–77	Glenn Pitt	Elderton
1978–79	Dennis Pennington	Bruin
1980–81	Kenneth Davis	Homer City
1982–83	William Linnon	Petersburg
1984–85	Lawrence C. Geortz	Parker
1986–87	Edward E. Pakes	Clymer
1988–89	James A. McCurdy	Reynoldsville
1990–91	Fred Zaugg	Cowansville
1992–93	William Bowers	Clarksburg

TWENTY-EIGHTH DISTRICT COMMANDERS
ELK, FOREST, MERCER, VENANGO, AND WARREN COUNTIES

1919	Norman M. Hulings	Oil City
	E. T. Dickey	Oil City
1920	Louis T. Cuthbert	Ridgway
1921	C. A. Kramer	Oil City
1922	C. Emerson Metzger	Warren
1923	George T. VanAken	Ridgway
1924–25	M. G. Miller	Mercer
1927	B. L. Keenan	Johnsonburg
1928	C. A. Kramer	Oil City
1929	Benjamin Kinnear	Warren
1930	William G. Smith	Grove City
1931	Fred Kearns	Franklin
1932	Charles A. Struble	Warren
1933	LeRoy Strauessley	Johnsonburg
1934	J. A. Minnin	Franklin
1935–36	Earl E. Siple	Greenville
1937	John A. Minnin	Franklin
1938	R. R. Hutton	Greenville
1939–40	Dick Hansen	Warren
1941–42	Maurice F. MacDonald	Ridgway
1943	Joseph F. Osenider	Oil City
1944	Walter S. Alexander	Sharpville
1945	Ralph W. McClintock	Johnsonburg
1946	A. L. Gillette	Oil City
1947	William G. Porter	Grove City
1948	Ralph M. McClintock	Johnsonburg
1949	Charles Cozad	Franklin
1950	Chester B. Dicks	Sharon
1951	Harry P. Anderson	Ridgway
1952	George Stewart	Oil City
1953	Raymond B. Gamble	Greenville
1954	Peter Straub	St. Mary's
1955	Henry Danielson	Pittsfield
1956	Thomas Nelson	Oil City
1957	Francis A. Masson	Sharon
1958	Alden Stearns	Sugar Grove

1959	James H. McMurray	St. Mary's
1960	Roy Dunkel, Jr.	Franklin
1961	Homer C. Alexander	Fredonia
1962	Marshall D. Stanton	Kinzua
1963	Daniel O. Connell	Johnsonburg
1964	Harry Ausel	Rouseville
1965	Warren Morgan	Sharon
1966	Merle A. Trumbull	Sugar Grove
1967	Martin G. Grunthaner	St. Mary's
1968	Clarence E. Miller	
1969	Albert W. Hendrickson	
1970	Conrad Ross	
1971	Lester Poinelli	Kersey
1972	Charles H. Cozad	Franklin
1973	David Cusick	Wheatland
1974	Carl V. Hornstrom	Youngsville
1975	Walter H. Shield, Sr.	Ridgway
1976	John Mackintosh	Oil City
1977	Frank A. Tucci	Farrell
1978	William Braughler	Warren
1979	Victor C. Straub	St. Mary's
1980	Richard B. Morrison	Franklin
1981	Paul L. Smith	Masury, Ohio
1982	Lester Poinelli	Kersey
1983	Jack Mackintosh	Oil City
1984	Merlin F. Jenkins	Pulaski
1985–86	George B. Eckert	St. Mary's
1987–88	Joseph D. Vannoy	Farrell
1989–90	Walter Staffin	Sharon
1991–92	Scott Barber	Youngsville
1992–93	Dennis Plotner	Sharpsville

TWENTY-NINTH DISTRICT COMMANDERS
CRAWFORD AND ERIE COUNTIES

1919	Elmer Hess	Erie
	Lucius M. Phelps	Erie
	Leo M. Hough	Meadville
	J. L. Kennedy	Meadville
1920	R. B. Stillman	Meadville
1921–23	Leland J. Culbertson	Meadville
1924–25	Clark O. Taynton	Erie
1926–28	Dr. R. B. McCord	Northeast
1929–30	Jesse Julianti	Erie
1931–32	Harold E. Whitford	Titusville
1933–37	Lloyd Stowe	Corry
1938–39	Henry Brown	Meadville
1940–41	Floyd B. Owens	Erie
1942–43	Sydney F. DeVore	Meadville
1944–45	Andress Frazier	Erie
1946–47	Henry T. Wheeler	Cambridge Springs
1948–49	Alfred D. Cook	Northeast
1950–51	Edward L. Beauchat	Titusville
1952–53	Don Allshouse	Erie
1954–55	Richard M. Horner	Cochrantown
1956–57	John Sedor	Erie
1958–59	Glen G. Hayes	Linesville
1960–61	William Ogsbury	Erie
1962–63	Elmer N. Nelson	Meadville
1964–65	Frank A. Borkowski	Erie
1966–67	David M. Willett	Erie
1968–69	Ira Garwood	
1970–71	Clarence W. Decker	Waterford
1972–73	William J. Sova	Erie
1974–75	Margaret C. Golden	Erie
1976	James R. Hookins	Titusville
1977–79	Clarence Winton	Titusville
1980–81	Leon E. Briggs	Waterford
1982–83	Evert Pringle	Cambridge Springs
1984–85	William A. Sidman, Jr.	Erie
1986–87	Lawrence R. Hock	Meadville

1988–89	Paul Shaffer	Girard
1990–91	Clare E. Blakeslee	Union City
1992–93	Paul E. Slayton	Cambridge Springs

THIRTIETH DISTRICT COMMANDERS
CARBON, MONROE, AND NORTHAMPTON COUNTIES

1919	Kenneth J. Kressler	Easton
	James B. Reilly	Easton
	Robert Singer	Stroudsburg
	Hugh Samsal	Stroudsburg
1920	Norman L. Piel	Easton
1921	B. F. Rosenberry	Palmerton
1922	Dr. J. J. Bellas	Lansford
1923	Earl A. Ziegenfus	Bethlehem
1924–26	Vere J. Banks	Stroudsburg
1927–28	Harry Sutton	Easton
1929–30	Harry Harman	Easton
1931–32	Oliver Frantz	Summit Hill
1933	Leo Achterman	Stroudsburg
1934	Montgomery F. Crowe	Stroudsburg
1935–36	John E. Helwick	Easton
1937–38	Clayton Williams	Lansford
1939–40	Chet Rogers	Easton
1941–42	Griffith H. Lloyd	East Stroudsburg
1943–44	William J. Newhart	Mauch Chunk
1945–46	Art Anders	Hellertown
1947–48	Willard Price	Canadensis
1949–50	Edwin H. Stickler	Lansford
1951–52	Kenneth S. Mack	Easton
1953–54	Elmer Heffer	East Stroudsburg
1955–56	Theodore Hinger	Jim Thorpe
1957–58	Ellsworth Palmer	Easton
1959–60	Melvin B. McElwain	East Stroudsburg
1961–62	James Nothstein	Lehighton
1963–64	Donald McPherson	Hellertown
1965–66	Herman Smeltz	East Stroudsburg
1967–68	Edward Kennedy	Summit Hill
1969–70	Richard Davey	
1971–72	Bernard E. Varvel	Canadensis
1973–74	Dawson Brown	Lehighton
1975–76	Allen Fretz	Nazareth
1977–78	James D. Shafer	East Stroudsburg

1979–80	William A. Schlecht	Jim Thorpe
1981–82	John J. Parry	Bangor
1983–84	Herman R. Smeltz	East Stroudsburg
1985–86	Harry J. Wynn III	Lehighton
1987–88	Michael Mudri, Jr.	Bethlehem
1989–90	Ralph E. Strunk, Sr.	Stroudsburg
1991–92	Jack R. Terry	Lansford
1992–93	Robert S. Moriarty	Bethlehem

THIRTY-FIRST DISTRICT COMMANDERS
WESTMORELAND COUNTY

1919	Richard Coulter	Greensburg
	Henry Coulter	Greensburg
1920	C. A. Thompson	Mount Pleasant
1921	Joseph Whitman	Jeannette
1922–25	Harry L. Fidler	Mount Pleasant
1926–29	John McCormick	Greensburg
1930–31	J. Guy Griffith	New Kensington
1932–33	John McMahon	Monessen
1934–36	Edward Stirling	Vandergrift
1937–39	Fred Trescher	Greensburg
1940–41	S. Wesley Hewlings	New Florence
1942–43	John W. Kinsey	Jeannette
1944–45	Ralph O. Byars	Scottdale
1946–47	Nick Roy	Greensburg
1948–49	H. S. Bitner	Latrobe
1950–51	Sherman W. Mason	Jeannette
1952–53	J. V. Vanderscott	Wyano
1954–55	Albert Kozak	Mount Pleasant
1956–57	Edward T. Hoak	Manor
1958–59	Joseph Boerio	Latrobe
1960–61	Dominic Davanti	Jeannette
1962–63	David Minto	Trafford
1964–65	Robert L. Frederick	Greensburg
1966–67	James W. Flowers	Latrobe
1968–69	Steve Mikosky	Jeannette
1970–71	Robert Joyner	Derry
1972–73	Frank Rzepniak	Ruffsdale
1974–75	Chesney Smith	Acme
1976–77	L. G. Smith	Latrobe
1978–79	James Leichliter	New Kensington
1980–81	Joe Rudnik	Mount Pleasant
1982–83	John Kolonay	Trafford
1984–85	Floyd Sheasley	Manor
1986–87	Max Licina	Trafford
1988–89	Frank Chinnici	Irwin
1990–91	Edward F. Steck	Latrobe
1992–93	Charles E. Achtzehn	McKeesport

THIRTY-SECOND DISTRICT COMMANDERS
ALLEGHENY COUNTY

1919	A. K. McRae	Pittsburgh
	Alex Loughlin	Pittsburgh
	Fred Hill	Pittsburgh
	John A. Graham	Pittsburgh
	Benjamin Metz	Pittsburgh
	F. D. Armstrong	Pittsburgh
	C. B. Mehard	Pittsburgh
	Walter P. Smart	Pittsburgh
1920	Dr. S. M. Rinehart	Sewickley
1921	William F. McFall	Pittsburgh
1922	J. Leo Collins	East Pittsburgh
1923–32	Charles G. Lane	Pittsburgh
1933–36	Charles P. Grimm	Pittsburgh
1937–38	Robert C. Malcolm	Curtisville
1939–40	William H. Turner	Pittsburgh
1941–42	John P. McAndress	Pittsburgh
1943–44	Joseph A. McKay	Allison Park
1945–46	Ben Schwab	Pittsburgh
1947–48	Rev. Francis Hoffman	Etna
1949–50	Frank X. Roache	Pittsburgh
1951–52	William L. Reder	Pittsburgh
1953–54	Harry G. Beck	Pittsburgh
1955–56	W. Raymond Jones	Glenshaw
1957–58	Samuel H. Sarraf	Pittsburgh
1959–60	Daniel A. Drew	Pittsburgh
1961–62	W. W. Foster	Pittsburgh
1962	William Bowers	
1963–64	William F. J. Cortright	Pittsburgh
1965–66	John M. Marcinko	Pittsburgh
1967–68	James H. Harvey	
1969–70	Robert L. Cornman	Pittsburgh
1971–72	Lee A. Shaw	Pittsburgh
1973–74	James P. Comiskey	Pittsburgh
1975–76	Charles R. Merriman	Sewickley
1977–78	Clifford T. Slaney	Pittsburgh
1979–80	Kathryn Bostedo	Saltsburg

1981–82	Robert Simpson	Sharpsburg
1983–84	George P. Keast	Pittsburgh
1985	Raymond Eicholtz	Bellevue
1985–86	George Lichaur, Jr.	Pittsburgh
1987–88	George Bostedo	Saltsburg
1989–90	William G. Outly	Pittsburgh
1991–92	David E. Cobaugh	Pittsburgh
1992–93	Albert Schraepfer	Avalon

THIRTY-THIRD DISTRICT COMMANDERS
ALLEGHENY COUNTY

1919	John Egloff	East Pittsburgh
	Leo A. Ivory	East Pittsburgh
	Leo Collins	East Pittsburgh
1920	Dr. S. M. Rinehart	Pittsburgh
1921	William C. McFall	Pittsburgh
1922	J. Leo Collins	East Pittsburgh
1923–25	Samuel McCahill	Pittsburgh
1926–29	John J. Deller	Wilmerding
1930–31	Dr. Herbert Dewar	Elizabeth
1932–35	T. B. Petty	McKeesport
1936–37	H. D. Croushore	East McKeesport
1938–39	Russell Shephard	Swissvale
1940–41	Michael F. Fisher	Swissvale
1942–43	Ben H. Byers	Elizabeth
1944–45	Leonard J. Bradley	Braddock
1946–47	Roy E. Thomas	Pittsburgh
1948–49	Peter J. Hubert	Turtle Creek
1950–51	Edwin M. Maxwell	Tarentum
1952–53	James M. Jackson	Turtle Creek
1954–55	Ralph E. Nicholas	Brackenridge
1956–57	Edward S. Richey	Natrona
1958–59	Homer E. Wertz	Pitcairn
1960–61	Stanley K. Jankovek	East Pittsburgh
1962–63	Charles Cope	McKeesport
1964–65	Henry Yurek	North Braddock
1966–67	Robert L. Coughlin	McKeesport
1968–69	Edward M. Slepsky	Wilmerding
1970–71	Edwin D. Stetz	Glassport
1972–73	William E. Gregory	Pittsburgh
1974–75	Guy R. Eisenhower	Port Vue
1976–77	Robert D. Goss, Jr.	McKeesport
1978–79	Jay E. Long	Pittsburgh
1980–81	Patrick F. Mullaney	North Versailles
1982–83	Raymond Crowell	East McKeesport
1984–85	John Glenwright	Monroeville
1986–87	Charles W. Watts	Pitcairn

1988–89	Glenn L. Lower	McKeesport
1990–91	Richard Wolfe	East Pittsburgh
1992–93	Rocco D. Ross	Pitcairn

THIRTY-FOURTH DISTRICT COMMANDERS
ALLEGHENY COUNTY

1919	Joseph Walsh	Pittsburgh
	R. L. Test	Pittsburgh
	William C. Arthur	Pittsburgh
	C. S. Shadle	Pittsburgh
	Carl A. Newcomber	Pittsburgh
1920	Dr. S. M. Rinehart	Sewickley
1921	William B. McFall	Pittsburgh
1922	J. Leo Collins	East Pittsburgh
1923	Jesse L. Nave	Pittsburgh
1924–25	E. P. Hayes	Pittsburgh
1926	E. P. Hayes	Pittsburgh
	Mary Welsh	Pittsburgh
1927–28	W. W. Hague	Library
1929–38	Thomas Thorntor.	Pittsburgh
1939–40	Dan C. Hartbauer	Pittsburgh
1941–42	George See	New Kensington
1943–44	C. C. Kellenberg	Pittsburgh
1945–46	J. T. Garbett	Pittsburgh
1947–48	F. M. Martin	Pittsburgh
1949–50	Alex Viggiano	Pittsburgh
1951–52	Thomas Pillion	Pittsburgh
1953–54	James E. Huff	Pittsburgh
1955–56	John E. Williams	Pittsburgh
1957–58	Regis F. Cusick, Jr.	Pittsburgh
1959–60	L. Edward Corlett	Pittsburgh
1961–62	Nicholas Diulus	Pittsburgh
1963–64	Andrew Demont	Pittsburgh
1965–66	Bernard J. Flinn	Pittsburgh
1967–68	Elmer L. Williams	Pittsburgh
1969–70	Steve Retorick	
1971–72	Harry Bauer	Pittsburgh
1973–74	Okley McGriff	Pittsburgh
1975–76	George M. Tarasovic	Pittsburgh

District Realigned

THIRTY-FIFTH DISTRICT COMMANDERS
ALLEGHENY COUNTY

1919	F. R. Flood	Pittsburgh
	Howard Rigby	Pittsburgh
	B. L. Succopp	Pittsburgh
	H. M. Becker	Pittsburgh
	Stuart Dunn	Pittsburgh
	Joseph H. Bialas	Pittsburgh
	Alan Donnelly	Pittsburgh
	Frank Miller	Pittsburgh
	George M. Hosack	Pittsburgh
1920	Dr. S. M. Rinehart	Sewickley
1921	William F. McFall	Pittsburgh
1922	J. Leo Collins	East Pittsburgh
1923–27	C. C. Benz	Pittsburgh
1928–37	Silas Waddell	East Liberty
1938–39	Ed Crump	East Liberty
1940–41	Salvatore Cancelliere	Pittsburgh
1942–43	Frank J. Boehm	Pittsburgh
1944–45	Charles Bartsch	Pittsburgh
1947	Conrad A. Eibeck	Pittsburgh
1948–49	John P. Coogan	Pittsburgh
1950–51	James P. Zargan	Pittsburgh
1952–53	Salvatore Cancelliere	Pittsburgh
1954–55	John R. Simmons	Pittsburgh
1956–57	John J. Pendergast	Pittsburgh
1958–59	William A. Comorado	Pittsburgh
1960–61	Henry R. Woods	Pittsburgh
1962–63	Joseph F. Watson	Pittsburgh
1964–65	John Ozanich	Pittsburgh
1966–67	Arch M. Beacom	Pittsburgh
1968–69	Leo L. Koppel	
1970–71	Joseph Stribling	Pittsburgh
1972–73	Guy K. Morris	Pittsburgh
1974–75	Edward J. Glackin	Pittsburgh
1976–77	Jack Haines	Monroeville
1978–79	Michael J. Meztk, Jr.	Pittsburgh
1980–81	James Kelly	Pittsburgh

1982–83	Okley McGriff	Pittsburgh
1984–85	Richard Cummings	Pittsburgh
1986–87	Aleck Attanucci	Pittsburgh
1988–89	William J. Corbett	Pittsburgh
1990–91	George Schurer	Gibsonia
1992–93	Michael Murphy	Pittsburgh

THIRTY-SIXTH DISTRICT COMMANDERS
ALLEGHENY COUNTY

1919	D. P. Foster	Carnegie
1920	Dr. S. M. Rinehart	Pittsburgh
1922	J. Leo Collins	East Pittsburgh
1923–26	Walter Grimm	Pittsburgh
1927–32	George Grimm	Pittsburgh
1933–38	John B. Nicklas	Pittsburgh
1939–40	Charles Ziegenfus	Pittsburgh
1941–42	Lawrence Trainor	Duquesne
1943–44	George C. Dietrich	Castle Shannon
1945–46	Frank Slocum	Homestead
1947–48	William R. McWilliams	Brentwood
1949–50	Harry V. Bair	McKees Rocks
1951–52	Laurence Walther	Bridgeville
1953–54	Charles Bunting	Homestead
1955–56	Daniel F. Cook	Pittsburgh
1957–58	George Cutler	Pittsburgh
1959–60	Angelo Pennetti	Bridgeville
1961–62	Edward Huth	Pittsburgh
1963–64	Rudolph F. Ferber	Pittsburgh
1965–66	Edward F. Fischer	Coraopolis
1967–68	David Pritchard	Pittsburgh
1969–70	Frank Spreha	
1971–72	Joseph D. Kelly	Pittsburgh
1973–74	Robert W. Wood	Bethel Park
1975–76	Frederick F. Felix	Pittsburgh
1977–78	Clare Brevard	Bethel Park
1979–80	Rodney Temple	Pittsburgh
1981–82	Ronald F. Conley	Pittsburgh
1983–84	Charles A. Caito	Pittsburgh
1985–86	Frederick C. Bigley	Pittsburgh
1987–88	Kenneth G. Dahner	Pittsburgh
1989–90	Norman Kappler	Bethel Park
1991–92	Howard R. McBride	Clairton
1992–93	Harold S. Stein	Pittsburgh

INDEX

227